GW01465839

TRAFALGAR

A TALE

BY

B. PEREZ GALDÓS

Author of "Gloria," etc.

FROM THE SPANISH BY CLARA BELL

AUTHORIZED EDITION

REVISED AND CORRECTED IN THE UNITED STATES

Vet. Span. III A

NEW YORK
WILLIAM S. GOTTSBERGER, PUBLISHER
London: Trübner & Co., 57 & 59 Ludgate Hill
PARIS: GALIGNANI, 224 RUE DE RIVOLI
1884

This edition is published expressly
for circulation in Europe
by authority of B. Perez Galdós

18508

Entered according to Act of Congress, in the year 1884 ·
BY WILLIAM S. GOTTSBERGER
in the Office of the Librarian of Congress, at Washington

TAYLOR INSTITUTION
UNIVERSITY
27 AUG 1969
OF OXFORD
LIBRARY

Press of
William S. Gottsberger
New York

TRAFALGAR.

CHAPTER I.

I TRUST that, before relating the important events of which I have been an eye-witness, I may be allowed to say a few words about my early life and to explain the singular accidents and circumstances which resulted in my being present at our great naval catastrophe.

In speaking of my birth I cannot follow the example of most writers who narrate the facts of their own lives, and who begin by naming their ancestry — usually of noble rank, *hidalgos* at the very least, if not actually descended from some royal or imperial progenitor. I cannot grace my opening page with high-sounding names, for, excepting my mother whom I remember for some few years, I know nothing of any of my fore-fathers, unless it be Adam from whom my descent would seem to be indisputable. In short, my his-

tory began in much the same way as that of
Pablos, the brigand of Segovia; happily it pleased
God that it should resemble it in no other particu-
lar.

I was born at Cadiz in the notorious quarter
" de la Viña," which was not then, any more than
at the present day, a good school of either morals
or manners. My memory does not throw any
light on the events of my infancy till I was six
years old, and I remember that, only because I
associate the idea of being six with an event I
heard much talked about, the battle of Cape St.
Vincent, which took place in 1797.

Endeavoring to see myself as I was at that
time, with the curiosity and interest which must
attach to self-contemplation, I am aware of a dim
and hazy little figure in the picture of past events,
playing in the creek with other small boys of the
same age, more or less. This was to me the whole
of life — as it was, at any rate, to our privileged
class; those who did not live as I did appeared to
me exceptional beings. In my childish ignorance
of the world I firmly believed that man was made
for the sea, Providence having created him to
swim as being the noblest exercise of his limbs
and body, and to dive for crabs as the highest use
of his intelligence — and especially to fish up and

sell the highly-esteemed crustacean known as
Bocas de la Isla — as well as for his personal de-
lectation and enjoyment, thus combining pleasure
with profit.

The society into which I was born was indeed
of the roughest, as ignorant and squalid as can
well be imagined; so much so that the boys of
our quarter of the town were regarded as even
lower than those of the adjoining suburb of Puntales, whose occupations were the same and who
defied the elements with equal devilry; the result
of this invidious distinction was that each party
looked upon the other as rivals, and the opposing
forces would meet from time to time for a pitched
battle with stones, when the earth was stained
with heroic blood.

When I was old enough to begin to think that
I might go into business on my own account, with
a view to turning an honest penny, I remember
that my sharpness stood me in good stead on the
quay where I acted as *valet de place* to the
numerous English who then, as now, disembarked
there. The quay was a free academy peculiarly
fitted to sharpen the wits and make the learner
wide-awake, and I was not one of the least apt
of its disciples in that wide branch of human experience; nor did I fail to distinguish myself in

petty thefts, especially of fruit, an art for which
the Plaza de San Juan offered an ample field, both
for the experiments of the beginner and the ex-
ploits of the adept. But I have no wish to enlarge
on this part of my history, for I blush with shame
now, as I remember the depth to which I had
sunk, and I thank God for having released me
from it at an early period, and directed me into a
better path.

Among the impressions which remain most
vivid in my memory is the enthusiastic delight I
felt at the sight of vessels of war, when they an-
chored outside Cadiz or in the cove of San Fernando. As I had no means of satisfying my
curiosity, when I saw these enormous structures I
conceived the most absurd and fanciful ideas about
them, imagining them as full of mysteries.

Always eager to mimic the greater world
around us, we boys too had our squadrons of little
ships, roughly hewn in wood, with sails of paper
or of rag, which we navigated with the greatest
deliberation and gravity in the pools of Puntales
or La Caleta. To make all complete, whenever a
few coppers came into our hands, earned by one or
another of our small industries, we bought powder
of old "Aunt Coscoja" in the street "del Torno
de Santa María," and with this we could have a

grand naval display. Our fleets sailed before the
wind in an ocean three yards across, fired off their
cannon, came alongside of each other to mimic a
hand-to-hand fight—in which the imaginary
crews valiantly held their own, and swarmed into
the tops unfurling the flag, made of any scrap of
colored rag we could pick up in a dust-heap—
while we danced with ecstasy on the shore at the
popping of the artillery, imagining ourselves to be
the nationalities represented by our respective
standards, and almost believing that in the world
of grown-up men and great events the nations too
would leap for joy, looking on at the victories of
their splendid fleets. Boys see things through
strange windows.

Those were times of great sea-fights, for there
was one at least every year and a skirmish every
month. I thought that fleets met in battle simply
and solely because they enjoyed it, or to prove
their strength and valor, like two bullies who meet
outside the walls to stick knives into each other.
I laugh when I recollect the wild ideas I had about
the persons and events of the time. I heard a
great deal about Napoleon and how do you think
I had pictured him to myself! In every respect
exactly like the smugglers whom we not unfrequently saw in our low quarter of the town:

Contrabandistas from the lines at Gibraltar. I
fancied him a man on horseback, on a Xerez nag,
with a cloak, high boots, a broad felt-hat, and a
blunderbuss of course. With these accoutrements,
and followed by other adventurers on the same
pattern, I supposed this man, whom all agreed in
describing as most extraordinary, to have conquered Europe, which I fancied was a large island
within which were other islands which were the
different nations: England, Genoa, London,
France, Malta, the land where the Moors lived,
America, Gibraltar, Port Mahon, Russia, Toulon
and so forth. This scheme of geography I had
constructed on the basis of the names of the
places from which the ships came whose passen-
gers I had to deal with; and I need not say that
of all these nations or islands Spain was the very
best, for which reason the English — men after the
likeness of highwaymen — wanted to get it for
their own. Talking of these and similar matters
I and my amphibious companions would give
vent to sentiments and opinions inspired by the
most ardent patriotism.

However, I need not weary the reader with
trifles which relate only to my personal fancies, so
I will say no more about myself. The one living
soul that made up to me for the wretchedness of

life by a wholly disinterested love for me, was my mother. All I can remember of her is that she was extremely pretty, or at any rate she seemed so to me. From the time when she was left a widow she maintained herself and me by doing washing, and mending sailors' clothes. She must have loved me dearly. I fell ill of yellow fever which was raging in Andalusía and when I got well she took me solemnly to mass at the old cathedral and made me kneel on the pavement for more than an hour, and then, as an *ex-voto* offering, she placed an image in wax of a child, which I believed to be an exact likeness of myself, at the foot of the altar where the service had been performed.

My mother had a brother, and if she was pretty, he was ugly and a cruel wretch into the bargain. I cannot think of my uncle without horror, and from one or two occurrences which I remember vividly I infer that this man must have committed some crime at the time I refer to. He was a sailor; when he was on shore and at Cadiz he would come home furiously drunk, and treat us brutally — his sister with words, calling her every abusive name, and me with deeds, beating me without any reason whatever.

My mother must have suffered greatly from

her brother's atrocities, and these, added to severe labor for miserable pay, hastened her death which left an indelible impression on my feelings, though the details dwell but vaguely in my memory. During this period of misery and vagabondage my only occupations were playing by the sea-shore or running about the streets. My only troubles were a beating from my uncle, a frown from my mother, or some mishap in the conduct of my squadrons. I had never felt any really strong or deep emotion till the loss of my mother showed me life under a harder and clearer aspect than it had ever before presented to me. The shock it gave me has never faded from my mind. After all these years I still remember, as we remember the horrible pictures of a bad dream, that my mother lay prostrate from some sickness, I know not what; I remember women coming and going, whose names and purpose I cannot recall; I remember hearing cries of lamentation, and being placed in my mother's arms, and then I remember the shudder that ran through my whole body at the touch of a cold, cold hand. I think I was then taken away; but mixed up with these dim memories I can see the yellow tapers which gave a ghastly light at mid-day, I can hear the muttering of prayers, the hoarse whispers of

the old gossips, the laughter of drunken sailors —
and then came the lonely sense of orphanhood, .
the certainty that I was alone and abandoned in
the world, which for a time absorbed me entirely.

I have no recollection of what my uncle was
doing at that time; I only know that his brutality
to me increased to such a point that, weary of his
cruelty, I ran away, determined to seek my fortune.
I fled to San Fernando and from thence to Puerto
Real. I hung on to the lowest class that haunt
the shore, which has always been a famous nest
for gaol-birds. Why or wherefore I quite forget,
but I found myself with a gang of these choice
spirits at Medinasidonia when, one day, a tavern
where we were sitting was entered by a press-
gang and we promptly separated, each hiding
himself as best he might. My good star led me
to a house where the owners had pity on me, taking the greatest interest in me, no doubt by
reason of the story I told, on my knees and
drowned in tears, of my miserable plight, my
past life and all my misfortunes.

These good people took me under their protection and saved me from the press-gang, and
from that time I remained in their service. With
them I went to Vejer de la Frontera where they

lived; they had only been passing through Medinasidonia.

My guardian angels were Don Alonso Gutier-rez de Cisniega, a ship's captain, and his wife, both advanced in years. They taught me much that I did not know, and as they took a great fancy to me before long I was promoted to be Don Alonso's page, accompanying him in his daily walks, for the worthy veteran could not use his right arm, and it was with difficulty that he moved his right leg. What they saw in me to arouse their inter-est I do not know; my tender years, my desolate circumstances and no doubt too my ready obedi-ence may have contributed to win their benevo-lence, for which I have always been deeply grate-ful. I may also add—though I say it that should not—as explaining their kind feeling towards me, that although I had always lived among the low-est and most destitute class, I had a certain natural refinement of mind which enabled me very soon to improve in mannèrs, and in a few years, notwithstanding I had no opportunities for learning, I could pass for a lad of respectable birth and training.

I had spent four years in this home when the events happened which I must now relate. The reader must not expect an accuracy of detail

which is out of my power when speaking of events
which happened in my tender youth, to be
recalled in the evening of my existence when I
am near the end of a long and busy life and already feel the slow poison of old age numbing the
fingers that use the pen; while the torpid brain
strives to cheat itself into transient return of
youth, by conjuring up the sweet or ardent
memories of the past. As some old men strive to
revive the warm delights of the past by gazing at
pictures of the beauties they have known, I will try
to give some interest and vigor to the faded
reminiscences of my long past days, and to warm
them with the glow of a counterfeit presentment of
departed glories.

The effect is magical! How marvellous are
the illusions of fancy! I look back with curiosity
and astonishment at the bygone years, as we look
through the pages of a book we were reading, and
left with a leaf turned down to mark the place;
and so long as the charm works I feel as if some
beneficent genius had suddenly relieved me of the
weight of old age, mitigating the burden of years
which crushes body and spirit alike. This blood
—this tepid and languid ichor, which now scarcely
lends warmth and life to my failing limbs, grows
hot again, flows, boils, and fires my veins with a

swifter course. A sudden light breaks in upon
my brain, giving color and relief to numberless
strange figures—just as the traveller's torch, blaz-
ing in some dark cavern, reveals the marvels of
geology so unexpectedly that it seems as though
they were then and there created. And my heart
rises from the grave of past emotions—a Lazarus
called by the voice of its Lord—and leaps in my
breast with joy and pain at once.

I am young again; time has turned backwards,
I stand in the presence of the events of my boy-
hood; I clasp the hands of old friends, the joys
and griefs of my youth stir my soul once more—
the fever of triumph, the anguish of defeat, intense
delights, acute sorrows—all crowded and mixed
in my memory as they were in life. But stronger
than any other feeling one reigns supreme, one
which guided all my actions during the fateful
period between 1805 and 1834. As I approach
the grave and reflect how useless I am among
men—even now tears start to my eyes with the
sacred love of country. I can only serve it with
words—cursing the base scepticism which can
deny it, and the corrupt philosophy which can treat
it as a mere fashion of a day.

This was the passion to which I consecrated
the vigor of my manhood, and to this I will de-

vote the labors of my last years, enthroning it as
the tutelary genius, the guiding spirit of my story
as it has been of my existence. I have much to
tell. Trafalgar, Bailén, Madrid, Zaragoza, Gerona,
Arapiles!—I can tell you something of all these,
if your patience does not fail. My story may not
be as elegantly told as it should be but I will do
my best to insure its being true.

CHAPTER II.

It was on one of the early days of October in that fatal year, 1805, that my worthy master called me into his room and looked at me with the severity that was habitual to him — a severity that was only on the surface for his nature was gentleness itself — he said :

" Gabriel, are you a brave man ?"

I did not know what to answer, for, to tell the truth, in my fourteen years of life no opportunity had ever presented itself for me to astonish the world with any deed of valor; still, it filled me with pride to hear myself called a man, and thinking it ill-judged to deny myself the credit of courage before any one who held it in such high estimation, I answered, with boyish boldness:

" Yes, sir, I am a brave man."

At this the noble gentleman, who had shed his blood in a hundred glorious fights and who nevertheless did not disdain to treat a faithful servant with frank confidence, smiled at me kindly, signed to me to take a seat, and seemed on the point of informing me of some business of importance, when his wife, my mistress, Doña Francisca entered the study, and, to give further interest to the discussion, began to declaim with vehemence.

"You are not to go," she said, "I declare you shall not join the fleet. What next will you be wanting to do? — at your age and when you have long retired as superannuated! No, no, Alonso my dear. You are past sixty and your dancing days are over."

I can see her now, that respectable and indignant dame — with her deep-bordered cap, her muslin dress, her white curls, and a hairy mole on one side of her chin. I describe these miscellaneous details, for they are inseparable from my recollection of her. She was pretty even in old age, like Murillo's Santa Anna, and her sober beauty would have justified the comparison if only the lady had been as silent as a picture. Don Alonso somewhat cowed, as he always was, by her flow of words, answered quietly:

"I must go, Paquita. From the letter I have just now received from my worthy friend Churruca, I learn that the united squadrons are either to sail from Cadiz and engage the English or to wait for them in the bay in case they are so bold as to enter. In either case it will be no child's play."

"That is well, and I am glad to hear it," replied Doña Francisca. "There are Gravina, Valdés, Cisneros, Churruca, Alcalá Galiano, and Alava ; let them pound away at the English dogs. But you are a piece of useless lumber who can do no good if you go. Why you cannot move that left arm which they dislocated for you at Cape St. Vincent."

My master lifted his arm, with a stiff attempt at military precision, to show that he could use it. But his wife, not convinced by so feeble an argument, went on with shrill asseveration.

" No, you shall not go, what can they want of a piece of antiquity like you. If you were still forty as you were when you went to Tierra del Fuego and brought me back those green Indian necklaces. — Then indeed ! But now ! — I know, that ridiculous fellow Marcial fired your brain this morning with talking to you about battles. It seems to me that Señor Marcial and I will come to quarrelling. — Let him go to the ships if he likes and pay them out for the foot he lost ! Oh ! Saint Jöseph the blessed ! If I had known when I was a girl what you sea-men were ! Endless worry ; never a day's peace ! A woman marries to live with her husband and one fine day a dispatch comes from Madrid and he is sent off at two minutes notice to the Lord knows where — Patagonia or Japan or the infernal regions. For ten or twelve months she sees nothing of him and at last, if the savages have not eaten him meanwhile, he comes back again the picture of misery — so ill and yellow that she does not know what to do to restore him to his right color. But old birds are not to be caught in a trap, and then suddenly another dispatch comes from Madrid, with orders to go to Toulon or Brest or Naples — go here and go there — wherever it is necessary to meet the whims of that rascally First Consul. . . .! If you would all do as I say, you would soon pay out these gentlemen who keep the world in a turmoil!"

My master sat smiling and gazing at a cheap print, badly colored by some cheap artist, which was nailed against the wall, and which represented the Emperor Napoleon mounted on a green charger, in the celebrated "redingote" which was smeared with vermilion. It was no doubt the sight of this work of art, which I had seen daily for four years, which had modified my ideas with respect to the smuggler's costume of the great man of the day, and had fixed his image in my mind as dressed something like a cardinal and riding a green horse.

"This is not living!" Doña Francisca went on, throwing up her arms: "God forgive me, but I

hate the sea, though they say it is one of His most
glorious works.   What is the use of the Holy In-
quisition, will you tell me, if it is not to burn
those diabolical ships of war to ashes ?   What is
the good of this incessant firing of cannon,— balls
upon balls, all directed against four boards, as you
may say, which are soon smashed to leave hun-
dreds of hapless wretches to drown in the sea ? Is
not that provoking God ?—And yet you men are
half-wild as soon as you hear a cannon fired !
Merciful Heaven ! my flesh creeps at the sound,
and if every one was of my way of thinking, we
should have no more sea-fights, and the cannon
would be cast into bells.   Look here, Alonso," she
said, standing still in front of her husband, " it
seems to me that they have done you damage
enough already; what more do you want ?   You
and a parcel of madmen like yourself,— had you
not enough to satisfy you on the 14th ?"*

Don Alonso clenched his fists at this bitter
reminiscence, and it was only out of consideration
for his wife, to whom he paid the utmost respect,
that he suppressed a good round oath.

" I lay all the blame of your absurd determination to join the fleet to that rascally Marcial,"

---

* The battle of Cape St. Vincent was fought on February 14, 1797.

the lady went on, warming with her own elo-quence; "that maniac for the sea who ought to have been drowned a hundred times and over, but that he escaped a hundred times to be the torment of my life. If he wants to join, with his wooden leg, his broken arm, his one eye, and his fifty wounds—let him go, by all means, and God grant he may never come back here again—but you shall not go, Alonso, for you are past service and have done enough for the King who has paid you badly enough in all conscience. If I were you, I would throw those captain's epaulettes you have worn these ten years in the face of the Generalis-simo of the land and sea forces. My word! they ought have made you admiral, at least; you earned that when you went on that expedition to Africa and brought me back those blue beads which I gave with the Indian necklace to decorate the votive urn to the Virgin 'del Cármen.'"

"Admiral or not, it is my duty to join the fleet, Paquita," said my master. "I cannot be absent from this struggle. I feel that I must pay off some of my arrears to the English."

"Do you talk of paying off arrears!" ex-claimed my mistress; "you—old, feeble, and half-crippled..."

2 *

"Gabriel will go with me," said Don Alonso, with a look at me which filled me with valor.

I bowed to signify that I agreed to this heroic scheme, but I took care not to be seen by my mistress, who would have let me feel the full weight of her hand if she had suspected my belli- cose inclinations. Indeed, seeing that her hus- band was fully determined, she was more furious than ever, declaring that if she had to live her life again nothing should induce her to marry a sailor. She cursed the Emperor, abused our re- vered King, the Prince of Peace, and all those who had signed the Treaty of Subsidies, ending by threatening the brave old man with punishment from Heaven for his insane rashness.

During this dialogue, which I have reported with approximate exactness as I have to depend on my memory, a loud barking cough in the ad- joining room revealed the fact that Marcial, the old sailor, could overhear with perfect ease, my mistress's vehement harangue, in which she had so frequently mentioned him in by no means flatter- ing terms. Being now desirous of taking part in the converstion, as his intimacy in the house fully justified his doing, he opened the door and came into Don Alfonso's room. Before going any farther I must give some account of my master's

former history, and of his worthy wife, that the
reader may have a better understanding of what
follows.

CHAPTER III.

Don Alfonso Gutierrez de Cisniega belonged to an old family of Vejer, where he lived. He had been devoted at an early age to a naval career and, while still quite young, had distinguished himself in defending Havana against the English in 1748. He was afterwards engaged in the expedition which sailed from Cartagena against the Algerines in 1775, and was present at the attack upon Gibraltar under the Duke de Crillon in 1782. He subsequently joined the expedition to the Straits of Magellan in the corvette *Santa María de la Cabeza*, commanded by Don Antonio de Córdova, and fought in the glorious engagements between the Anglo-Spanish fleet and the French before Toulon in 1793, terminating his career of glory at the disastrous battle of Cape St. Vincent, where he commanded the *Mejicano*, one of the ships which were forced to surrender.

From that time my master, whose promotion had been slower than his laborious and varied career had merited, retired from active service. He suffered much in body from the wounds he

had received on that fatal day, and more in mind
from the blow of such a defeat. His wife nursed
and tended him with devotion though not in
silence, for abuse of the navy and of seamen of
every degree were as common in her mouth as
the names of the saints in that of a bigot.

Doña Francisca was an excellent woman, of
exemplary conduct and noble birth, devout and
God-fearing — as all women were in those days,
charitable and judicious, but with the most violent
and diabolical temper I ever met with in the
whole course of my life. Frankly I do not
believe that this excessive irritability was natural
to her, but the result and outcome of the worries
in her life arising out of her husband's much-hated
profession; it must be confessed that she did not
complain wholly without reason, and every day
of her life Doña Francisca addressed her prayers
to Heaven for the annihilation of every fleet in
Europe. This worthy couple had but one child,
a daughter — the incomparable Rosita, of whom
more anon.

The veteran, however, pined sadly at Vejer,
seeing his laurels covered with dust and gnawed
to powder by the rats, and all his thoughts and
most of his discourse, morning, noon, and night,
were based on the absorbing theme that if Cór-

dova, the commander of the Spanish fleet, had only given the word "Starboard" instead of "Port" the good ships *Mejicano, San José, San Nicolás* and *San Isidro* would never have fallen into the hands of the English, and Admiral Jervis would have been defeated. His wife, Marcial, and even I myself, exceeding the limits of my duties— always assured him that there was no doubt of the fact, to see whether, if we acknowledged ourselves convinced, his vehemence would moderate— but no; his mania on that point only died with him.

Eight years had passed since that disaster, and the intelligence that the whole united fleet was to fight a decisive battle with the English had now roused my master to a feverish enthusiasm which seemed to have renewed his youth. He pictured to himself the inevitable rout of his mortal enemies; and although his wife tried to dissuade him, as has been said, it was impossible to divert him from his wild purpose. To prove how obstinate his determination was it is enough to mention that he dared to oppose his wife's strong will, though he avoided all discussion; and to give an adequate idea of all that his opposition implied I ought to mention that Don Alonso was afraid of no mortal thing or creature—neither of the English, the French, nor the savages of Magellan, not of the angry sea, nor of the monsters of the deep, nor of the raging tempest, nor of anything in the earth or sky—but only of his wife.

The last person I must mention is Marcial the sailor, the object of Doña Francisca's deepest aversion, though Don Alonso, under whom he had served, loved him as a brother.

Marcial—no one knew his other name—called by all the sailors "the Half a Man," had been boatswain on various men-of-war for forty years. At the time when my story begins this maritime hero's appearance was the strangest you can imagine. Picture to yourself an old man, tall rather than short, with a wooden leg, his left arm shortened to within a few inches of the elbow, minus an eye, and his face seamed with wounds in every direction — slashed by the various arms of the enemy; with his skin tanned brown, like that of all sea-faring men, and a voice so hoarse, hollow and slow, that it did not seem to belong to any rational human creature, and you have some idea of this eccentric personage. As I think of him I regret the narrow limits of my palette, for he deserves painting in more vivid colors and by a worthier artist. It was hard to say whether his appearance was most calculated

to excite laughter or command respect — both at
once I think, and according to the point of view
you might adopt.

His life might be said to be an epitome of the
naval history of Spain during the last years of the
past century and the beginning of this—a history
in whose pages the most splendid victories alternate with the most disastrous defeats. Marcial
had served on board the *Conde de Regla*, the *San
Joaquin*, the *Real Cárlos*, the *Trinidad* and other
glorious but unfortunate vessels which, whether
honorably defeated or perfidiously destroyed, carried with them to a watery grave the naval power
of Spain. Besides the expeditions in which my
master had taken part Marcial had been present
at many others, such as that of Martinica, the
action of Cape Finisterre, and before that the
terrible battle close to Algeciras in July, 1801,
and that off Cape Santa María on the 5th of October, 1804. He quitted the service at sixty-six
years of age, not however for lack of spirit but
because he was altogether "unmasted" and past
fighting. On shore he and my master were the
best of friends, and as the boatswain's only daugh -
ter was married to one of the servants of the
house, of which union a small child was the token,
Marcial had made up his mind to cast anchor for

good, like a hulk past service, and even succeeded in making himself believe that peace was a good thing. Only to see him you would have thought that the most difficult task that could be set to this grand relic of a hero was that of minding babies; but, as a matter of fact, Marcial had no other occupation in life than carrying and amusing his grandchild, putting it to sleep with his snatches of sea-songs, seasoned with an oath or two — excusable under the circumstances.

But no sooner had he heard that the united fleets were making ready for a decisive battle than his moribund fires rose from their ashes, and he dreamed that he was calling up the crew in the forecastle of the *Santísima Trinidad.* Discovering in Don Alfonso similar symptoms of rejuvenescence, he confessed to him, and from that hour they spent the chief part of the day and night in discussing the news that arrived and their own feelings in the matter; "fighting their battles o'er again," hazarding conjectures as to those to be fought in the immediate future, and talking over their day-dreams like two ship's boys indulging in secret visions of the shortest road to the title of Admiral.

In the course of these *tête-à-tête* meetings, which occasioned the greatest alarm to Doña

Francisca, the plan was hatched for setting out to join the fleet and be present at the impending battle. I have already told the reader what my mistress's opinion was and all the abuse she lavished on the insidious sailor; he knows too that Don Alonso persisted in his determination to carry out his rash purpose, accompanied by me, his trusty page, and I must now proceed to relate what occurred when Marcial himself appeared on the scene to take up the cudgels for war against the shameful *status quo* of Doña Francisca.

CHAPTER IV.

"SEÑOR MARCIAL," she began, with increased indignation, " if you choose to go to sea again and lose your other hand, you can go if you like; but my husband here, shall not."

"Very good," said the sailor who had seated himself on the edge of a chair, occupying no more space on it than was necessary to save himself from falling: "I will go alone. But the devil may take me if I can rest without looking on at the fun!"

Then he went on triumphantly: "We have fifteen ships and the French twenty smaller vessels. If they were all ours we should not want so many. Forty ships and plenty of brave hearts on board!"

Just as the spark creeps from one piece of timber to the next, the enthusiasm that fired Marcial's one eye lighted up both my master's, though dimmed by age. " But the *Señorito*" (Lord Nelson), added the sailor, " will bring up a great many men too. That is the sort of performance I enjoy: plenty of timbers to fire at, and plenty of gunpowder-smoke to warm the air when it is cold."

I forgot to mention that Marcial, like most sailors, used a vocabulary of the most wonderful and mongrel character, for it seems to be a habit among seamen of every nation to disfigure their mother tongue to the verge of caricature. By examining the nautical terms used by sailors we perceive that most of them are corruptions of more usual terms, modified to suit their eager and hasty temperament trained by circumstances to abridge all the functions of existence and particularly speech. Hearing them talk it has sometimes occurred to me that sailors find the tongue an organ that they would gladly dispense with.

Marcial, for instance, turned verbs into nouns and nouns into verbs without consulting the authorities. He applied nautical terms to every action and movement, and identified the ideas of a man and a ship, fancying that there was some analogy between their limbs and parts. He would say in speaking of the loss of his eye that his larboard port-hole was closed, and explained the amputation of his arm by saying that he had been left minus his starboard cat-head. His heart he called his courage-hold and his stomach his bread-basket. These terms sailors at any rate could understand; but he had others, the offspring of his own inventive genius of which he alone understood the meaning or could appreciate the force. He had words of his own coining for doubting a statement, for feeling sad; getting drunk he always called "putting on your coat" among a number of other fantastical idioms; and the derivation of this particular phrase will never occur to my readers without my explaining to them that the English sailors had acquired among the Spaniards the nickname of "great-coats," so that when he called getting drunk "putting your coat on" a recondite allusion was implied to the favorite vice of the enemy. He had the most extraordinary nicknames for foreign admirals; Nelson he called the *Señorito*, implying a certain amount of respect for him; Collingwood was *Rio Calambre*, (Uncle Cramp) which he believed to be an equivalent for the English name; Jervis he called—as the English did too—The old Fox; Calder was known as *Rio Perol* (Uncle Boiler) from an association of the name Cálder with *caldera*, a kettle, and by an entirely different process he dubbed Villeneuve, the Admiral of the united fleets, with the name of *Monsieur Corneta*, borrowed from some play he had once seen acted at Madrid. In fact, when reporting the conversations I can recall, I must perforce translate his wonderful phraseology into more ordinary language, to avoid going into long and tiresome explanations.

To proceed, Doña Francisca, devoutly crossing herself, answered angrily:

"Forty ships! Good Heavens! it is tempting Providence; and there will be at least forty thousand guns for the enemies to kill each other."

"Ah! but *Monsieur Corneta* keeps the courage-hold well filled!" exclaimed Marcial, striking his breast. "We shall laugh at the great-coats this time. It will not be Cape St. Vincent over again."

"And you must not forget," added my master eagerly recurring to his favorite hobby, "that if Admiral Córdova had only ordered the *San José* and the *Mejicano* to tack to port, Captain Jervis would not now be rejoicing in the title of Earl St. Vincent. Of that you may be very certain, and I have ample evidence to show that if we had gone to port the day would have been ours."

"Ours!" exclaimed Doña Francisca scornfully. "As if you could have done more. To hear these fire-eaters it would seem as if they wanted to conquer the world, and as to going to sea—it appears that their shoulders are not broad enough to bear the blows of the English."

"No," said Marcial resolutely and clenching his fist defiantly. "If it were not for their cunning and knavery. . . .! We got out against them with a bold front, defying them like men, with our flag hoisted and clean hands. The English never sail wide, they always steal up and surprise us, choosing heavy seas and stormy weather. That is how it was at the Straits, when we were made to pay so dearly. We were sailing on quite confidingly, for no one expected to be trapped even by a heretic dog of a Moor, much less by an Englishman who does the polite thing in a Christian fashion.— But no, an enemy who sneaks up to fight is not a Christian — he is a highwayman. Well now, just fancy, señora," and he turned to Doña Francisca to engage her attention and good-will, "we were going out of Cadiz to help the French fleet which was driven into Algeciras by the English. — It is four years ago now, and to this day it makes me so angry that my blood boils as I think of it. I was on board the *Real Cárlos*, 112 guns, commanded by Ezguerra, and we had with us the *San Hermenegildo*, 112 guns too, the *San Fernando*, the *Argonáuta*, the *San Agustin*, and the frigate *Sabina*. We were joined by the French squadron of four men-of-war, three frigates and a brigantine, and all sailed out of Algeciras for Cadiz at twelve o'clock at noon; and as the wind was slack when night fell we were close under Punta Carnero. The night was blacker than a barrel of pitch, but the weather was fine so we could hold on our way in spite of the darkness. Most of the crew were asleep; I remember, I was sitting in the fo'castle talking to the mate, Pepe Débora, who was telling me all the dog's tricks his mother-in-law had played him, and alongside we could see the lights of the *San Hermenegildo*, which was sailing at a gun-shot to starboard. The other ships were ahead of us. For the very last thing we any of us thought of was that the 'great-coats' had slipped out of Gibraltar and were giving chase — and how the devil should we, when they had doused all their lights and were stealing up to us without our guessing it? Suddenly, for all that the night was so dark, I fancied I saw something — I always had a port-light like a lynx — I fancied a ship was standing between us and the *San Hermenegildo*. 'José Débora,' says I, 'either I saw a ghost or there is an Englishman to starboard?' José Débora looks himself, and then he says: 'May the main-mast go by the board,' says he, 'if there is e'er a ship to starboard but the *San Hermenegildo*.' 'Well,' says I, 'whether or no I am going to tell the officer of the watch.'

"Well hardly were the words out of my mouth
when, rub-a-dub! we heard the tune of a whole
broadside that came rattling against our ribs. The
crew were on deck in a minute, and each man at
his post. That was a rumpus, señora! I wish you
could have been there, just to have an idea of how
these things are managed. We were all swearing
like demons and at the same time praying the
Lord to give us a gun at the end of every finger to
fight them with. Ezguerra gave the word to return their broadside. — Thunder and lightning!
They fired again, and in a minute or two we responded. But in the midst of all the noise and
confusion we discovered that with their first broadside they had sent one of those infernal combusti-
bles (but he called it 'comestibles') on board
which fall on the deck as if it were raining fire.
When we saw our ship was burning we fought like
madmen and fired off broadside after broadside.
Ah! Doña Francisca, it was hot work I can tell
you!—Then our captain took us alongside of the
enemy's ship that we might board her. I wish
you could have seen it! I was in my glory then;
in an instant we had our axes and boarding-pikes
out, the enemy was coming down upon us and my
heart jumped for joy to see it, for this was the
quickest way of settling accounts. On we go,

right into her!—Day was just beginning to dawn,
the yards were touching, and the boarding parties
ready at the gangways when we heard Spanish
oaths on board the foe.   We all stood dumb with
horror, for we found that the ship we had been
fighting with was the *San Hermenegildo* herself."

"That was a pretty state of things," said Doña
Francisca roused to some interest in the narrative.
"And how had you been such asses—with not a
pin to choose between you?"

"I will tell you.   We had no time for explanations then.   The flames on our ship went over to
the *San Hermenegildo* and then, Blessed Virgin!
what a scene of confusion.   'To the boats!' was
the cry.   The fire caught the *Santa Barbara* and
her ladyship blew up with loud explosion.—We
were all swearing, shouting, blaspheming God and
the Virgin and all the Saints, for that seems the
only way to avoid choking when you are primed
to fight, up to the very muzzle . . ."

"Merciful Heavens how shocking!" cried my
mistress.   "And you escaped?"

"Forty of us got off in the launch and six or
seven in the gig, these took up the second officer
of the *San Hermenegildo*.   José Débora clung to a
piece of plank and came to shore at Morocco,
more dead than alive."

" And the rest ?"

" The rest—the sea was wide enough to hold
them all. Two thousand men went down to
Davy Jones that day, and among them our captain, Ezguerra, and Emparan, the captain of the
other ship."

" Lord have mercy on them!" ejaculated Doña
Francisca. "Though God knows! they were but
ill-employed to be snatched away to judgment.
If they had stayed quietly at home, as God re-
quires . . . "

" The cause of that disaster," said Don Alonso,
who delighted in getting his wife to listen to these
dramatic narratives, "was this: The English emboldened by the darkness arranged that the Su-
perb, the lightest of their vessels, should extinguish
her lights and slip through between our two finest
ships. Having done this, she fired both her
broadsides and then put about as quickly as possible to escape the struggle that ensued. The
two men-of-war, finding themselves unexpectedly
attacked, returned fire and thus went on battering
each other till dawn, when, just as they were
about to board, they recognized each other and
the end came as Marcial has told you in detail."

" Ah! and they played the game well," cried

the lady. "It was well done though it was a mean trick!"

"What would you have?" added Marcial. "I never loved them much; but since that night!... If *they* are in Heaven I do not want ever to go there. Sooner would I be damned to all eternity!"

"Well—and then the taking of the four frigates which were coming from Rio de la Plata?" asked Don Alfonso, to incite the old sailor to go on with his stories.

"Aye—I was at that too," said Marcial. "And that was where I left my leg. That time too they took us unawares, and as it was in time of peace we were sailing on quietly enough, only counting the hours till we should be in port, when suddenly——I will tell you exactly how it all happened, Doña Francisca, that you may just understand the ways of those people. After the engagement at the Straits I embarked on board the *Fama* for Montevideo, and we had been out there a long time when the Admiral of the squadron received orders to convoy treasure from Lima and Buenos Ayres to Spain. The voyage was a good one and we had no mishaps but a few slight cases of fever which only killed off a few of our men. Our freight was heavy—gold belonging to the king and to private persons, and we also

had on board what we called the 'wages chest' —
savings off the pay of the troops serving in America. Altogether, if I am not much mistaken, a
matter of fifty millions or so of *pesos,* as if it were
a mere nothing; and besides that, wolf-hides,
vicuña wool, cascarilla, pigs of tin and copper,
and cabinet woods. Well, sir, after sailing for
fifty days we sighted land on the 5th of October,
and reckoned on getting into Cadiz the next day
when, bearing down from the northeast, what
should we see but four frigates. Although, as I
said, it was in time of peace, and though our captain, Don Miguel de Zapiain, did not seem to have
any suspicion of evil, I — being an old sea-dog —
called Débora and said to him that there was
powder in the air, I could smell it. Well, when
the English frigates were pretty near, we cleared
the decks for action; the *Fama* went forward and
we were soon within a cable's length of one of the
English ships which lay to windward.

"The English captain hailed us through his
speaking-trumpet and told us — there is nothing
like plain-speaking — told us to prepare to defend
ourselves, as he was going to attack. He asked
a string of questions, but all he got out of us was
that we should not take the trouble to answer
him. Meanwhile the other three frigates had

come up and had formed in such order that each
Englishman had a Spaniard to the leeward of
him."

"They could not have taken up a better position," said my master.

"So say I," replied Marcial. "The commander of our squadron, Don José Bustamante, was
not very prompt; if I had been in his shoes. . . .
Well, señor, the English commodore sent a little
whipper-snapper officer, in a swallow-tail coat, on
board the Medea, who wasted no time in trifling
but said at once that though war had not been
declared, the commodore had orders to take us.
That is what it is to be English! Well, we engaged at once; our frigate received the first
broadside in her port quarter; we politely returned the salute, and the cannonade was brisk
on both sides — the long and the short of it is
that we could do nothing with the heretics, for
the devil was on their side; they set fire to the
Santa Bárbara which blew up with a roar, and
we were all so crushed by this and felt so cowed
— not for want of courage, señor, but what they
call demoralized — well, from the first we knew
we were lost. There were more holes in our
ship's sails than in an old cloak; our rigging was
damaged, we had five feet of water in the hold,

our mizzen-mast was split, we had three shots in the side only just above the water line and many dead and wounded. Notwithstanding all this we went on, give and take, with the English, but when we saw that the *Medea* and the *Clara* were unable to fight any longer and struck their colors we made all sail and retired, defending ourselves as best we could. The cursed English-man gave chase, and as her sails were in better order than ours we could not escape and we had nothing for it but to haul our colors down at about three in the afternoon, when a great many men had been killed and I myself was lying half-dead on the deck, for a ball had gone out of its way to take my leg off. Those d——d wretches carried us off to England, not as prisoners, but as *détenus;* however, with despatches on one side and despatches on the other, from London to Madrid and back again, the end of it was that they stuck for want of money; and, so far as I was concerned, another leg might have grown by the time the King of Spain sent them such a trifle as those five millions of *pesos.*"

"Poor man! — and it was then you lost your leg ?" asked Doña Francisca compassionately.

"Yes, señora, the English, knowing that I was no dancer, thought one was as much as I could

want. In return they took good care of me. I
was six months in a town they called *Plinmuf*
(Plymouth) lying in my bunk with my paw tied
up and a passport for the next world in my
pocket.— However, God A'mighty did not mean
that I should make a hole in the water so soon;
an English doctor made me this wooden leg,
which is better than the other now, for the other
aches with that d———d rheumatism and this one,
thank God, never aches even when it is hit by a
round of small shot. As to toughness, I believe
it would stand anything, though, to be sure, I
have never since faced English fire to test it."

"You are a brave fellow," said my mistress.
"Please God you may not lose the other. But
those who seek danger . . ."

And so, Marcial's story being ended, the dis-
pute broke out anew as to whether or no my
master should set out to join the squadron. Doña
Francisca persisted in her negative, and Don
Alonso, who in his wife's presence was as meek
as a lamb, sought pretexts and brought forward
every kind of reason to convince her.

"Well we shall go to look on, wife, — simply
and merely to look on "— said the hero in a tone
of entreaty.

"Let us have done with sight-seeing," answered his wife. "A pretty pair of lookers-on you two would make!"

"The united squadrons," added Marcial, "will remain in Cadiz—and they will try to force the entrance."

"Well then," said my mistress, "you can see the whole performance from within the walls of Cadiz, but as for going out in the ships — I say no, and I mean no, Alonso. During forty years of married life you have never seen me angry (he saw it every day)—but if you join the squadron I swear to you . . . . remember, Paquita lives only for you!"

"Wife, wife—" cried my master much disturbed: "Do you mean I am to die without having had that satisfaction?"

"A nice sort of satisfaction truly! to look on at mad men killing each other! If the King of Spain would only listen to me, I would pack off these English and say to them: 'My beloved subjects were not made to amuse you. Set to and fight each other, if you want to fight.' What do you say to that?—I, simpleton as I am, know very well what is in the wind, and that is that the first Consul — Emperor—Sultan—whatever you call him — wants to settle the English, and as he has no men brave enough for the job he has im-

posed upon our good King and persuaded him to
lend him his; and the truth is he is sickening us
with his everlasting sea-fights. Will you just tell
me what is Spain to gain in all this? Why is
Spain to submit to being cannonaded day after
day for nothing at all? Before all that rascally
business Marcial has told us of what harm had the
English ever done us?—Ah, if they would only
listen to me! Master Buonaparte might fight by
himself, for I would not fight for him!"

"It is quite true," replied my master, "that
our alliance with France is doing us much damage, for all the advantages accrue to our ally,
while all the disasters are on our side."

"Well, then, you utter simpletons, why do
you encourage the poor creatures to fight in this
war?"

"The honor of the nation is at stake," replied
Don Alonso, "and after having once joined the
dance it would be a disgrace to back out of it.
Last month, when I was at Cadiz, at my cousin's
daughter's christening, Churruca said to me:
'This French alliance and that villainous treaty
of San Ildefonso, which the astuteness of Buonaparte and the weakness of our government made
a mere question of subsidies, will be the ruin of
us and the ruin of our fleet if God does not come

to the rescue, and afterwards will be the ruin of
the colonies too and of Spanish trade with America.   But we must go on now all the same. . .' "

"Well," said Doña Francisca, "what I say is
that the Prince of Peace is interfering in things
he does not understand.   There you see what a
man without learning is!   My brother the arch-
deacon, who is on Prince Ferdinand's side, says
that Godoy is a thoroughly commonplace soul,
that he has studied neither Latin nor theology
and that all he knows is how to play the guitar
and twenty ways of dancing a gavotte.   They
made him prime minister for his good looks, as it
would seem.   That is the way we do things in
Spain!   And then we hear of starvation and
want — everything is so dear — yellow fever
breaking out in Andalusia.— This is a pretty state
of things, sir, — yes, and the fault is yours;
yours," she went on, raising her voice and turning
purple.   "Yes, señor, yours, who offend God by
killing so many people — and if you would go to
church and tell your beads instead of wanting to
go in those diabolical ships of war, the devil
would not find time to trot round Spain so nim-
bly, playing the mischief with us all."

"But you shall come to Cadiz too," said Don
Alonso, hoping to light some spark of enthusiasm

in his wife's heart; "you shall go to Flora's house, and from the balcony you will be able to see the fight quite comfortably, and the smoke and the flames and the flags. — It is a beautiful sight!"

"Thank you very much — but I should drop dead with fright. Here we shall be quiet; those who seek danger may go there."

Here the dialogue ended, and I remember every word of it though so many years have elapsed. But it often happens that the most remote incidents that occurred even in our earliest childhood, remain stamped on our imagination more clearly and permanently than the events of our riper years when our reasoning faculties have gained the upper hand.

That evening Don Alonzo and Marcial talked over matters whenever Doña Francisca left them together; but this was at rare intervals, for she was suspicious and watchful. When she went off to church to attend vespers, as was her pious custom, the two old sailors breathed freely again as if they were two giddy schoolboys out of sight of the master. They shut themselves into the library, pulled out their maps and studied them with eager attention; then they read some papers in which they had noted down the names of several English vessels with the number of their guns and men,

and in the course of their excited conference, in
which reading was varied by vigorous commen-
tary, I discovered that they were scheming the
plan of an imaginary naval battle. Marcial, by
means of energetic gymnastics with his arm and a
half, imitated the advance of the squadron and the
explosion of the broadsides; with his head he
indicated the alternate action of the hostile vessels;
with his body the heavy lurch of each ship as it
went to the bottom; with his hand the hauling
up and down of the signal flags; he represented
the boatswain's whistle by a sharp sibilation; the
rattle of the cannon by thumping his wooden leg
on the floor; he smacked his tongue to imitate
the swearing and confusion of noises in the fight;
and as my master assisted him in this performance
with the utmost gravity I also must need take my
share in the fray, encouraged by their example
and giving natural vent to that irresistible longing
to make a noise which is a master passion with
every boy. Seeing the enthusiasm of the two
veterans, I could no longer contain myself and
took to leaping about the room — a freedom in
which I was justified by my master's kind famili-
arity; I imitated with my head and arms the
movements of a vessel veering before the wind,
and at the same time making my voice as big as

possible I shouted out all the most sonorous monosyllables I could think of as being most like the noise of a cannon. My worthy master and the mutilated old sailor, quite as childish as I in their own way, paid no attention to my proceedings, being entirely preoccupied with their own ideas.

How I have laughed since when I have remembered the scene! and how true it is — in spite of all my respect for my companions in the game — that senile enthusiasm makes old men children once more and renews the puerile follies of the cradle even on the very brink of the tomb!

They were deep in their discussion when they heard Doña Francisca's step returning from church.

"She is coming!" cried Marcial in an agony of alarm, and they folded up the maps and began to talk of indifferent matters. I, however, not being able to cool down my juvenile blood so rapidly or else not noticing my mistress's approach soon enough, went on, down the middle of the room in my mad career, ejaculating with the utmost incoherence, such phrases as I had picked up: "Tack to starboard! Now Port! Broadside to the leeward! Fire! Bang! bom! boom!..." She came up to me in a fury and without any warning delivered a broadside on my figure-head with her right hand, and with such effect that for a few moments I saw nothing but stars.

"What! you too?" she cried, battering me unmercifully. "You see," she added, turning on her husband with flashing eyes, "you have taught him to feel no respect for you!—You thought you were still in the *Caleta* did you, you little ne'er do weel?"

The commotion ended by my running off to the kitchen crying and disgraced, after striking my colors in an ignominious manner, before the superior force of the enemy; Doña Francisca giving chase and belaboring my neck and shoulders with heavy slaps. In the kitchen I cast anchor and sat down to cry over the fatal termination of my sea-fight.

TAYLOR INST OXFORD

CHAPTER V.

In opposing her husband's insane determination to join the fleet, Doña Francisca did not rely solely on the reasons given in the last chapter; she had another and more weighty one which she did not mention in the course of that conversation, perhaps because it was wiser not. But the reader does not know it, and must be told.

I have mentioned that my master had a daughter; this daughter's name was Rosita; she was a little older than I was, that is to say scarcely fifteen, and a marriage had been arranged for her with a young officer of artillery named Malespina, belonging to a family of Medinasidonia and distantly related to my master. The wedding had been fixed for the end of October and, as may be supposed, the absence of the bride's father on so solemn an occasion would have been highly improper.

I must here give some account of my young lady, of her bridegroom, her love-affairs and her projected marriage; and alas! my recollections take a tinge of melancholy, recalling to my fancy

many troublesome and far-away scenes, figures
from another world — and stirring my weary old
heart with feelings of which I should find it hard
to say whether they were more pleasurable or sad.
Those ardent memories which now lie withered in
my brain, like tropical flowers exposed to a chill
northern blast, sometimes make me laugh — but
sometimes make me grave. However, to my tale,
or the reader will be tired of these wearisome
reflections which, after all, interest no one but
myself.

Rosita was uncommonly pretty. I remember
vividly how pretty she was, though I should find
it difficult to describe her features. I fancy I see
her now, smiling in my face; the curious expression of her countenance, unlike any other I ever
saw, dwells in my mind — from the perfect dis-
tinctness with which it rises before me — like one
of those innate ideas which seem to have come
into the world with us from a former existence, or
to have been impressed on our minds by some
mysterious power while we were still in the cradle.
And yet I cannot describe it, for what then was
real and tangible remains now in my brain as a
vague ideal; and while nothing is so fascinating
as a beloved ideal, nothing so completely eludes
all categorical description.

4 *

When I first went into the house I thought that Rosita belonged to some superior order of beings; I will explain my feelings more fully that you may form an idea of my utter simpleness. When we are little and a child comes into the world within our family the grown-up folks are apt to tell us that it has come from France, Paris, or England. I, like other children, having no notions as to the multiplication of the human race, firmly believed that babies were imported packed up in boxes like a cargo of hardware. Thus, gazing for the first time at my master's daughter, I argued that so lovely a being could not have come from the same factory as the rest of us, that is to say from Paris or from England, and I remained convinced that there must be some enchanted region where heaven-sent workmen were employed in making these choicer and lovelier specimens of humanity. Both of us being children, though in different ranks of life, we were soon on those terms of mutual confidence which were natural to our years, and my greatest joy was in playing with her, submitting to all her vagaries and insolence, which is not saying a little, for our relative position was never lost sight of in our games; she was always the young lady and I always the servant, so that I got the worst of it when slaps were going, and I need not say who was the sufferer.

My highest dream of happiness was to be allowed to fetch her from school, and when, by some unforeseen accident, some one else was entrusted with this delightful duty I was so deeply distressed that I honestly thought there could be no greater grief in life, and would say to myself: "It is impossible that I should ever be more miserable when I am a man grown." My greatest delight was to climb the orange-tree in the courtyard to pick the topmost sprays of blossom; I felt myself at a height far above the greatest king on earth when seated on his throne, and I can remember no pleasure to be compared to that of being obliged to capture her in that divinely rapturous game known as hide and seek. If she ran like a gazelle I flew like a bird to catch her as soon as possible, seizing her by the first part of her dress or person that I could lay my hand on. When we changed parts, when she was the pursuer and I was to be caught, the innocent delight of the blissful game was doubled, and the darkest and dingiest hole in which I might hide, breathlessly awaiting the grasp of her imprisoning hands, was to me a perfect paradise. And I may honestly say that during these happy games I never had a thought or a feeling that did not emanate from the purest and most loyal idealism.

Then her singing! From the time when she was quite little she used to sing the popular airs of Andalusia with the ease of a nightingale, which knows all the secrets of song without having been taught. All the neighbors admired her wonderful facility and would come to listen to her, but to me their applause and admiration were an offence; I could have wished her to sing to no one but me. Her singing was a sort of melancholy warbling, qualified by her fresh childlike voice. The air, which repeated itself with complicated little turns and trills like a thread of sound, seemed to be lost in distant heights and then to come back to earth again on the low notes. It was like the song of the lark as it rises towards heaven and suddenly comes down to sing close in our ears; the spirit of the hearer seemed to expand as it followed the voice, and then to contract again, but always following the swing of the melody and feeling the music to be inseparable from the sweet little singer. The effect was so singular that to me it was almost painful to hear her, particularly in the presence of others.

We were, as I have said, of about the same

age, she being eight or nine months older than I was. But I was stunted and puny while she was well grown and vigorous, and at the end of my three years' residence in the house she looked much the elder of the two. These three years slipped by without our either of us suspecting that we were growing up; our games went on without interruption, for she was much livelier by nature than I, though her mother would scold her, trying to keep her in order and make her study—in which, however, she did not always succeed. At the end of these three years, however, my adored young mistress was a woman grown; her figure was round and well formed, giving the finishing touch to her beauty; her face had a tenderer blush, a softer form, a gentler look; her large eyes were brighter but their glance was less restless and eager; her gait was more sober; her movements were, I cannot say lighter nor less light, but certainly different, though I could not, either then or now, define in what the difference lay. But no change struck me so much as that in her voice, which acquired a gravity and depth very unlike the shrill gay tones in which she had been wont to call me, bewildering my common-sense and making me leave my various duties to join in her games. The bud, in short, had become a rose, the chrysalis was transformed into a butterfly.

Then, one day — one dreadful, dismal day — my young mistress appeared before me in a long dress. This alteration made such an impression on me that I could not speak a word the whole day. I felt like a man who has been cruelly imposed upon, and I was so vexed with her that in my secret soul I found fifty reasons for seriously resenting her rapid development. A perfect fever of argumentativeness was fired in my brain, and I debated the matter with myself in the most fervent manner during my sleepless nights. The thing that utterly confounded me was that the addition of a few yards of stuff to her skirts seemed altogether to have altered her character. That day — a thousand times unblessed — she spoke to me with the greatest formality, ordering me coldly and even repellently to do all the things I least liked doing — and she, who had so often been my accomplice and screen in idleness, now reproved me for it! and all this without a smile, or a skip, or a glance! — No more running, no more songs, no more hiding for me to find her, no making believe to be cross ending in a laugh — not a squabble, not even a slap from her sweet little hand! It was a terrible crisis

in my life — she was a woman and I was still a
child !

I need not say that this was an end to our
pranks and games; I never again climbed the
orange-tree, which henceforth blossomed unmo-
lested by my greedy devotion, and unfolded its
leaves and shed its luscious perfume at its own
sweet will; we never again scampered across the
court-yard, nor trotted too and from school — I,
so proud of my responsibility, that I would have
defended her against an army if they had tried to
carry her off. From that day Rosita always
walked with the greatest dignity and circumspec-
tion. I often observed that as she went up-stairs
in front of me she took care not to show an inch,
not a line, of her pretty ankles, and this systematic
concealment I felt to be an insult to my dignity,
for I had till lately seen a great deal more than
her ankles! Bless me! I can laugh now when I
remember how my heart was ready to burst over
these things.

But worse misfortunes were in store. One day
in the same year as that of this transformation old
'Aunt' Martina, Rosario the cook, Marcial, and
other members of the kitchen society were discussing something very important. I made the
best use of my ears and presently gathered the

most alarming hints: My young mistress was to
be married. The thing seemed incredible for I
had never heard of a lover. However, the parents
used to arrange all these matters and the strange
thing is that sometimes they did not turn out
badly. A young man of good family had asked
her hand, and her parents had consented. He
came to the house accompanied by his relatives,
who were some kind of counts or marquises with
a high-sounding title. The suitor wore a naval
uniform, for he served his country as a sailor, but
in spite of his elegant costume he was by no
means attractive. This no doubt was the impression he made on my young mistress, for from the
first she manifested a great dislike to the marriage.
Her mother tried to persuade her, but all in vain
though she drew the most flattering picture of the
young man's excellent talents, ancient lineage and
splendid wealth. The young girl was not to be
convinced, and answered all these arguments with
others no less cogent.

However, the sly baggage never said a word
about the real reason, which was that she had
another lover whom she really loved. This was a
young artillery officer, Don Rafael Malespina, a
fine-looking young fellow with a pleasing face.
My young mistress had made his acquaintance in

church, and the traitor Love had taken advantage
of her while she was saying her prayers; but
indeed a church has always seemed the fittest
place, with its poetical and mysterious influences,
for the doors of the soul to be opened for the
admission of love. Malespina took to lurking
round the house, in which I detected him on
various occasions, and this love-affair became so
much talked of in Vejer that the young naval
officer came to know of it and challenged his rival.
My master and mistress heard the whole story
when news was brought to the house that Malespina had wounded his antagonist severely.

The scandal caused an immense commotion.
My mistress's religious feelings were so much
shocked by this deed that neither she nor my
master could conceal their wrath, and Rosita was
their first victim. However, months went by;
the wounded man got well again, and as Malespina himself was a man of birth and wealth, there
were evident indications in the political atmosphere of the house that Don Rafael was about to
be admitted. The parents of the wounded man
gave up the suit, and those of the conqueror
appeared in their place to ask the hand of my
sweet young mistress. After some discussion and
demur the match was agreed upon.

I remember the first time old Malespina came.
He was a very tall, dry-looking man with a gau-
dily-colored waistcoat, a quantity of seals and
ornaments hanging to his watch, and a very large
sharp nose with which he seemed to be smelling
every one he talked to. He was terribly voluble
and never allowed any one else to get a word in;
he contradicted everything, and it was impossible
to praise anything without his saying that he had
something far better. From the first I felt sure
he was a vain man and utterly untruthful, and my
opinion was amply justified later. My master
received him with friendly politeness, as well as
his son who came with him. From that time the
lover came to the house every day, sometimes
alone and sometimes with his father.

Now a new phase came over my young mistress. Her coolness to me was so marked that it
verged on utter contempt. It made me understand clearly, for the first time, the humbleness of
my condition, and I cursed it bitterly; I tried to
argue with myself as to the claims to superiority
of those who really were my superiors, asking myself, with real anguish of mind, how far it was right
and just that others should be rich and noble and
learned, while my ancestry were of such low
origin; my sole fortune was my skin, and I hardly

knew how to read. Seeing what the reward of my devotion was, I fully believed that there was no ambition in this wide world that I dared aspire to ; and it was not till long after that I acquired a rational conviction that, by a steady and vigorous use of my own powers, I might gain almost everything I was deficient in. Under the scorn with which she treated me I lost all confidence in myself; I never dared open my lips in her presence, and she inspired me with far greater awe than her parents. Meanwhile I attentively watched all the signs of the love that possessed her; I saw her sad and impatient when her lover was late; at every sound of an approaching footstep her pretty face flushed and her black eyes sparkled with anxiety and hope. If it was he who came in she could not conceal her rapture, and then they would sit and talk for hours together; but always under the eye of Doña Francisca, for she would not have allowed the young lady to have a *tête-à-tête* meeting with any one, even through iron bars.

However, they carried on an extensive correspondence, and the worst of it all was that I had to be the go-between and courier. That drove me mad!—The regular thing was that I should go out and meet the young gentleman at a certain place, as punctually as a clock, and he would give me a note to carry to my young mistress; having discharged this commission, she would give me one to take to him. How often have I felt tempted to burn those letters instead of delivering them. However, luckily for me, I always kept cool enough to resist this base temptation. I need hardly add that I hated Malespina; I no sooner saw him come into the house than my blood boiled, and whenever he desired me to do anything I did it as badly and sulkily as possible, wishing to betray my extreme disgust. This disgust, which to them seemed simply bad service, while to me it was a display of honest wrath worthy of a proud and noble heart, earned me many reprimands, and above all it once led my young lady to make a speech that pierced me to the heart like the thrust of an arrow. On one occasion I heard her say: "That boy is getting so troublesome that we shall have to get rid of him."

At last the day was fixed for the wedding, and it was only a short while before that event that all I have already related took place with reference to my master's project. It may therefore be easily understood that Doña Francisca had excellent reasons for objecting to her husband's joining the fleet, besides her regard for his safety.

CHAPTER VI.

I REMEMBER very well that the day after the cuffing bestowed on me by Doña Francisca in her wrath at my irreverent conduct and her intense aversion to all naval warfare, I went out to attend my master in his daily walk. He leaned upon my arm, and on the other side of him walked Marcial; we went slowly to suit Don Alonso's feeble pace and the awkwardness of the old sailor's wooden leg. It was like one of those processions in which a group of tottering and worm-eaten saints are carried along on a shaky litter, threatening to fall if the pace of the bearers is in the least accelerated. The two old men had no energy or motive power left but their brave hearts, which still acted as truly as a machine just turned out of a workshop; or like the needle of a ship's compass which, notwithstanding its unerring accuracy, could do nothing to work the crazy craft it served to guide! During our walk my master—after having asserted, as usual, that if Admiral Córdova had only tacked to port instead of starboard the battle of 'the 14th' would never have been lost—turned the conversation once more on their grand project, and though they did not put their scheme into plain words, no doubt because I was present, I gathered from what they said that they intended to effect their purpose by stealth, quietly walking out of the house one morning without my mistress's knowledge.

When we went in again indifferent matters were talked over. My master, who was always amiable to his wife, was more so, that day, than ever. Doña Francisca could say nothing, however trivial, that he did not laugh at immoderately. He even made her a present of some trifles, doing his utmost to keep her in a good humor, and it was no doubt as a result of this conspicuous complaisance that my mistress was crosser and more peevish than I had ever seen her. No accommodation was possible; she quarrelled with Marcial over heaven knows what trifle, and desired him to quit the house that instant; she used the most violent language to her husband; and during dinner, though he praised every dish with unwonted warmth, the lady was implacable and went on grumbling and scolding.

At last it was time for evening prayers, a solemn ceremony performed in the dining-room in the presence of all the household; and my

master, who would not unfrequently go to sleep
while he lazily muttered the *Paternoster*, was that
evening unusually wide awake and prayed with
genuine fervor, his voice being heard above all
the rest. Another incident occurred which struck
me particularly. The walls of the rooms were
decorated with two distinct sets of prints : sacred
subjects and maps — the hierarchy of Heaven on
one hand and the soundings all round Europe and
America on the other. After supper my master
was standing in the passage, studying a mariner's
chart and tracing lines upon it with his trembling forefinger, when Doña Francisca, who had
gathered some hints of the plan for evasion, and
who always appealed to Heaven when she caught
her husband red-handed in any manifestations of
nautical enthusiasm, came up behind him, and
throwing up her arms, exclaimed :

"Merciful Heaven ! If you are not enough to
provoke a Saint !"

"But, my dear," my master timidly replied,
"I was only tracing the course taken by Alcalá
Galiano and Valdés in the schooners *Sutil* and
Mejicana when we went to explore the straits of
Magellan. It was a delightful expedition — I must
have told you all about it."

"I shall come to burning all that paper trash !"

cried Doña Francisca. "A plague on voyages and on the wandering dog of a Jew who invented them. You would do better to take some concern for the salvation of your soul, for the long and the short of it is you are no chicken. What a man! to be sure—what a man to have to take care of!"

She could not get over it; I happened to pass that way, but I cannot remember whether she relieved her fury by giving me a thrashing and demonstrating at once the elasticity of my ears and the weight of her hands. The fact is that these little endearments were so frequently repeated, that I cannot recollect whether I received them on this particular occasion; all I remember is that my master, in spite of his utmost amiability, entirely failed to mollify his wife.

Meanwhile I have neglected to speak of Rosita; she was in a very melancholy mood, for Señor de Malespina had not made his appearance all day nor written her a note; all my excursions to the market-place having proved vain. Evening came and with it grief fell on the young girl's soul, for there was no hope now of seeing him till next day — but suddenly, after supper had been ordered up, there was a loud knock at the door. I flew to open it, and it was he; before I opened it my hatred had recognized him.

I fancy I can see him now as he stood before me then, shaking his cloak which was wet with rain. Whenever I recall that man I see him as I saw him then. To be frankly impartial, I must say he was a very handsome young fellow, with a fine figure, good manners, and a pleasant expression; rather cold and reserved at first, grave and extremely courteous with the solemn and rather exaggerated politeness of the old school. He was dressed that evening in a frock-coat, with riding breeches and top boots; he wore a Portuguese hat and a very handsome cloak of scarlet cloth, lined with silk, which was the height of fashion with the gilded youth of that time.

As soon as he had come in I saw that something serious had happened. He went into the dining-room where all were much surprised to see him at so late an hour, for he never called in the evening; but my young mistress had hardly time to be glad before she understood that this unexpected visit was connected with some painful occasion.

"I have come to take leave of you," said Malespina. They all sat stupefied, and Rosita turned as white as the paper on which I am writing; then she turned scarlet and then again as pale as death.

5 *

"But what has happened? Where are you going Don Rafael?" asked my mistress. I have said that Malespina was an artillery officer, but I did not mention that he was stationed at Cadiz and at Veger only on leave.

"As the fleet is short of men," he replied, "we are under orders to embark and serve on board ship. They say a battle is inevitable and most of the vessels are short of gunners."

"Christ, Mother Mary and Saint Joseph!" shrieked Doña Francisca almost beside herself. "And they are taking you too? That is too much. Your duties are on land, my friend. Tell them to manage as best they may; if they want men let them find them. Upon my soul this is beyond a joke!"

"But, my dear," said Don Alonso humbly, "do not you see that they must . . . ." But he could not finish his sentence, for Doña Francisca, whose cup of wrath and grief was overflowing, proceeded to apostrophize all the potentates of the earth.

"You —" she exclaimed, "anything and everything seems right in your eyes, if only it is to benefit those blessed ships of war. And who, I say, who is the demon from hell who has ordered land forces on board ship? You need not tell me.—It is Buonaparte's doing. No Spaniard would have concocted such an infernal plot. Go and tell them that you are just going to be married. Come now," she added, turning to her husband, "write to Gravina and tell him that this young man cannot join the squadron." Then, seeing that her husband only shrugged his shoulders, she cried:

"He is of no use whatever! Mercy on me! If only I wore trousers I would be off to Cadiz and stop there till I had got you out of this mess."

Rosita said not a word. I who was watching her narrowly perceived how agitated she was. She never took her eyes off her lover, and if it had not been for good manners and to keep up her dignity, she would have cried and sobbed loudly to relieve the grief that was almost suffocating her.

"The soldier," said Don Alonso, "is the slave of duty, and our young friend is required by his country to serve on board ship in her defence. He will gain glory in the impending struggle, and make his name famous by some great deed which history will record as an example to future generations."

"Oh yes—this, that and the other!" said

Doña Francisca mimicking the pompous tone in which her husband had made this speech. "We know — and all for what? To humor those ne'er-do-weels at Madrid. Let them come themselves to fire the cannons, and fight on their own account!— And when do you start?"

"To-morrow morning. My leave is cut short and I am under orders to proceed at once to Cadiz."

It would be impossible to describe the look that came into my young mistress's face as she heard these words. The lovers looked at each other, and a long and mournful silence fell after this announcement of Malespina's immediate departure.

"But this is not to be borne!" exclaimed Doña Francisca. "They will be calling out the peasantry next — and the women too, if the whim takes them. Lord of Heaven!" she went on looking up to the ceiling with the glare of a pythoness, "I do not fear to offend Thee by saying: Curses on the inventor of ships — Curses on all who sail in them, and Curses on the man who made the first cannon, with its thunder that is enough to drive one mad, and to be the death of so many poor wretches who never did any harm!"

Don Alonso looked at the young officer, expecting to read some protest in his face against these insults to the noble science of gunnery. Then he said:

"The worst of it is that the ships will lack material too and it would be . . . ."

Marcial, who had been listening at the door to the whole conversation, could no longer contain himself. He came into the room saying:

"And why should they lack material ? — The *Trinidad* carries 140 guns — 32 thirty-six pounders, 34 twenty-four pounders, 36 twelve-pounders, 18 eighty-pounders, and 10 mortars. The *Príncipe de Asturias* carries 118, the *Santa Ana* 120, the *Rayo* 100, the *Nepomuceno*, and the *San* . . . ."

"What business have you to interfere!" exclaimed Doña Francisca. "And what does it matter to us whether they carry fifty or eighty ?" But Marcial went on with his patriotic list all the same, but in a lower voice and speaking only to my master, who dared not express his approbation. Doña Francisca went on:

"But for God's sake, Don Rafael, do not go. Explain that you are a landsman, that you are going to be married. If Napoleon must fight, let him fight alone: let him come forward and say: ' Here am I — kill me, you English — or let me kill you.' Why should Spain be subject to his lordship's vagaries?"

"I must admit," said Malespina, "that our alliance with France has proved most disastrous."

"Then why was it made? Every one says that this Godoy is an ignorant fellow. You might think a nation could be governed by playing the guitar!"

"After the treaty of Basle," the young man said, "we were forced to become the enemies of the English, who defeated our fleet off Cape St. Vincent."

"Ah! there you have it!" exclaimed Don Alonso, striking the table violently with his fist. "If Admiral Córdova had given the word to tack to port, to the vessels in front — in accordance with the simplest rules of strategy — the victory would have been ours. I consider that proved to a demonstration, and I stated my opinion at the time. But every man must keep his place."

"The fact remains that we were beaten," said Malespina. "The defeat might not have led to such serious consequences if the Spanish ministry had not signed the treaty of San Ildefonso with the French republic. That put us at the mercy of the First Consul, obliging us to support him in wars which had no aim or end but the furthering

of his ambition. The peace of Amiens was no
better than a truce ; England and France declared
war again immediately, and then Napoleon de-
manded our assistance. We wished to remain
neutral, for that treaty did not oblige us to take
any part in the second war, but he insisted on our
co-operation with so much determination that the
King of Spain, to pacify him, agreed to pay him a
subsidy of a hundred millions of *reales* — it was
purchasing our neutrality with gold. But even so
we did not get what we had paid for; in spite of
this enormous sacrifice we were dragged into war.
England forced us into it by seizing, without any
justification, four of our frigates returning from
America freighted with bullion. After such an
act of piracy the parliament of Madrid had no
choice but to throw the country into the hands of
Napoleon, and that was exactly what he wished.
Our navy agreed to submit to the decision of the
First Consul — nay, he was already Emperor —
and he, hoping to conquer the English by strata-
gem, sent off the combined fleets to Martinique, intending to draw off the British naval forces from
the coasts of Europe. Thus he hoped to realize
his favorite dream of invading Great Britain ; but
this clever trick only served to prove the inexperi-
ence and cowardice of the French Admiral who, on

his return to Europe would not share with our navy the glory of the battle off Finisterre. Then, in obedience to the Emperor's orders, the combined fleets were to enter Brest. They say that Napoleon is furious with the French Admiral and intends to supplant him immediately."

"But from what they say," Marcial began, putting his oar in again, as we say, "Monsieur Corneta wants to cancel it, and is on the look-out for some action which may wipe out the black mark against him. I am only too glad, for then we shall see who can do something and who cannot."

"One thing is certain," Malespina went on, "the English fleet is cruising in our waters and means to blockade Cadiz. The Spanish authorities think that our fleet ought not to go out of the bay, where they have every chance of conquering the foe; but it seems that the French are determined to go out to sea."

"We shall see," said my master. "It cannot fail to be a glorious battle, any way."

"Glorious! yes...." replied Malespina. "But who can promise that fortune shall favor us. You sailors indulge in many illusions and, perhaps from seeing things too closely, you do not realize the inferiority of our fleet to that of the English.

They, besides having a splendid artillery have all the materials at hand for repairing their losses at once. As to the men, I need say nothing. The enemy's sailors are the best in the world — all old and experienced seamen, while only too many of the Spanish vessels are manned by raw recruits, indifferent to their work and hardly knowing how to serve a gun; our marines, again, are not all we could wish, for they have been supplemented by land-forces — brave enough, no doubt, but certain to be sea-sick."

"Well, well," said my master, "in the course of a few days we shall know the end of it all."

"I know the end of it all very well," said Doña Francisca. "All these gentlemen — though I am far from saying they will not have gained glory — will come home with broken heads."

"What can you know about it?" exclaimed Don Alonso, unable to conceal an impulse of vexation, which, however, lasted but a moment.

"More than you do," she retorted sharply. "But God have you in his keeping, Don Rafael, that you may come back to us safe and sound."

This conversation had taken place during supper, which was a melancholy meal, and after Doña Francisca's last speech no one said another word. The meal ended, Malespina took a tender leave of

them all, and as a special indulgence on so solemn
an occasion the kind-hearted parents left the lovers
together, allowing them to bid each other adieu at
their ease and unseen, so that nothing might prevent their indulging in any demonstration which
might relieve their anguish. It is evident that I
was not a spectator of the scene and I know
nothing of what took place; but it may be supposed that no reticence on either side checked the
expression of their feelings.

When Malespina came out of the room he was
as pale as death ; he once more bid farewell to my
master and mistress, who embraced him affectionately, and was gone. When we went up to Rosita
we found her drowned in tears, and her grief was
so desperate that her devoted parents could not
soothe her by any persuasion or argument, nor revive her energy by any of the remedies for which
I was sent backwards and forwards to the apothe-
cary. I must confess that I was so deeply grieved
at the distress of these hapless lovers that my
rancorous feelings against Malespina died away in
my breast. A boy's heart is easily appeased, and
mine was always open to gentle and generous impulses.

CHAPTER VII.

THE following morning had a great surprise in store for me, and my mistress was thrown into the most violent passion I suppose she can ever have known in her life. When I got up I perceived that Don Alonso was in the best of humors, and his wife even more ill-tempered than usual. While she was gone to mass with Rosita, I saw my master packing in the greatest haste, putting shirts, and other articles of clothing, and among them his uniform, into a portmanteau. I helped him and it made me suspect that he was about to steal away; still, I was surprised to see nothing of Marcial. However, his absence was presently accounted for; for Don Alonso, having made his rapid arrangements, became extremely impatient till the old sailor made his appearance, saying: " Here is the chaise. Let us be off before she comes in." I took up the valise, and in a twinkling Don Alonso, Marcial, and I had sneaked out of the back gate so as to be seen by nobody; we got into the chaise, which set off as fast as the wretched hack could draw it and the badness of the road allowed.

This, which was bad enough for horses was almost impassable for vehicles; however, in spite of jolting that almost made us sick, we hurried as much as possible, and until we were fairly out of sight of the town our martyrdom was allowed no respite.

I enjoyed the journey immensely, for every novelty turns the brain of a boy. Marcial could not contain himself for joy, but my master, who at first displayed his satisfaction with even less reticence than I, became sadder and more subdued when we had left the town behind us. From time to time he would say: "And she will be so astonished! What will she say when she goes home and does not find us!"

As for me, my whole being seemed to expand at the sight of the landscape, with the gladness and freshness of the morning, and above all with the idea of soon seeing Cadiz and its matchless bay, crowded with vessels; its gay and busy streets and its creek (the Caleta) which remained in my mind as the symbol of the most precious gift of life — liberty; its Plaza, its jetty and other spots, all dear to my memory. We had not gone more than three leagues when there came in sight two riders mounted on magnificent horses, who were fast overtaking us and before long joined us.

We had at once recognized them as Malespina and
his father — the tall, haggard, and chattering old
man of whom I have already spoken. They were
both much surprised to see Don Alonso, and still
more so when he explained that he was on his way
to Cadiz to join a ship. The son took the announcement with much gravity; but the father,
who as you will have understood was an arrant
braggart and flatterer, complimented my master in
high-flown terms on his determination, calling him
the prince of navigators, the mirror of sailors, and
an honor to his country.

We stopped to dine at the inn at Conil. The
gentlemen had what they could get, and Marcial
and I eat what was left, which was not much. I
waited at table and heard the conversation, by
which means I gained a better knowledge of the
elder Malespina, who at first struck me as a boastful liar and afterwards as the most amusing chat-
terbox I ever in my life met with.

Don José Malespina, my young mistress's intended father-in-law — no relation to the famous
naval officer of that name — was a retired colonel
of artillery, and his greatest pride was founded on
his perfect knowledge of that branch of military
science and on his personal superiority in the tactics of gunnery. When he enlarged on that sub-

ject his imagination seemed to gain in vividness and in freedom of invention.

"Artillery," he said, without pausing for a moment in the act of deglutition, "is indispensable on board ships of war. What is a vessel without guns? But it is on land, Señor Don Alonso, that the marvellous results of that grand invention of the human mind are seen to the best advantage. During the war in Roussillon — you know of course that I took part in that campaign and that all our successes were due to my promptness in managing the artillery.—The battle of Masdeu—: How do you suppose that was won? General Ricardos posted me on a hill with four pieces, ordering me not to fire till he sent the word of command. But I, not taking the same view of the case, kept quiet till a column of the French took up a position in front of me, in such a way as that my fire raked them from end to end. Now the French troops form in file with extraordinary precision. I took a very exact aim with one of my guns, covering the head of the foremost soldier. — Do you see? The file was wonderfully straight. — I fired, and the ball took off one hundred and forty-two heads Sir! and the rest did not fall only because the farther end of the line swerved a little. This produced the greatest consternation among the enemy, but as they did not understand my tactics and could not see me from where they stood, they sent up another column to attack our troops on my right, and that column shared the same fate, and another and another, till I had won the battle."

"Well, señor, it was wonderful!" said my master, who, seeing the enormity of the lie, had no mind to trouble himself to contradict his friend.

"Then in the second campaign, under the command of the Conde de la Union, we gave the republicans a very pretty lesson. The defence of Boulou was not successful because we ran short of ammunition ; but in spite of that I did great damage by loading a gun with the keys of the church — however, they did not go far, and as a last and desperate resource I loaded the cannon with my own keys, my watch, my money, a few trifles I found in my pockets and, at last, with my decorations. The strange thing is that one of the crosses found its billet on the breast of a French general, to which it stuck as if it had been glued there and did him no harm whatever. He kept it, and when he went to Paris, the Convention condemned him to death or exile—I forget which— for having allowed himself to accept an order from the hand of an enemy."

6

"The devil they did !" said my master, highly
delighted with these audacious romances.

"When I was in England," continued the old
soldier, "you know of course, that I was sent for
by the English to make improvements in their
artillery,— I dined every day with Pitt, with
Burke, with Lord North, Lord Cornwallis, and
other distinguished personages, who always called
me 'the amusing Spaniard.' I remember that
once, when I* was at the Palace, they entreated
me to show them what a bull-fight was like and
I had to throw my cloak over a chair and to prick
it and kill it, which vastly diverted all the court,
and especially King George III., who was very
great friends with me, and was always saying that
I must send to my country to fetch some good.
olive-trees.   Oh ! we were on the best terms
possible.   All his anxiety was that I should teach
him a few words of Spanish, and above all some
of our beautiful Audulusian — but he could never
learn more than '*otro toro*' (another bull) and
'*vengan esos cinco*' (that makes five), and he
greeted me with these phrases every day when I
went to breakfast with him off pescadillas* and a
few *cañitas* of Manzanilla."

* Pescadillas are a small fish peculiar to the south Atlantic coast
of Spain. *Cañitas* is the name given to certain small glasses used
only for drinking Manzanilla.

"That was what he took for breakfast?"

"That was what he preferred. I had some pescadillas bottled and brought from Cadiz. They kept very well by a recipe I invented and have at home."

"Wonderful! And you succeeded in reforming the English artillery?" asked my master, encouraging him to go on for he was greatly amused.

"Perfectly. I invented a cannon which could never be fired, for all London, including the ministers and parliament, came to entreat me not to attempt it, because they feared that the explosion would throw down a number of houses."

"So that the great gun has been laid aside and forgotten?"

"The Emperor of Russia wanted to buy it, but it was impossible to move it from the spot where it stood."

"Then you surely can get us out of our present difficulties by inventing a cannon to destroy the whole English fleet at one discharge."

"Yes," replied Malespina. "I have been thinking of it, and I believe I may realize my idea. I will show you the calculations I have made, not only with regard to increasing the calibre of guns to a fabulous degree, but also for

constructing armor plates to protect ships and
bastions.   It is the absorbing idea of my life."

By this time the meal was ended.   Marcial
and I disposed of the fragments in less than no
time, and we set out again; the Malespinas on
horseback by the side of the chaise and we, as
before, in the tumble-down vehicle.   The effects
of the dinner, and of the copious draughts of
liquor with which he had moistened it, had stimu-
lated the old gentleman's inventive powers and
he went on all the way, pouring out a flood of
nonsense.   The conversation returned to the subject with which it had begun, the war in Roussillon,
and as Don José was preparing to relate fresh
deeds of valor, my master, weary of so many falsehoods, tried to divert him to something else, by
saying: "It was a disastrous and impolitic war.
We should have done better never to have under-
taken it."

"Oh! the Conde de Aranda, as you know,"
exclaimed Malespina, "condemned that unlucky
war with the Republic from the first.   How often
have we discussed the question — for we have
been friends from our childhood.   When I was
in Aragon we lived together for six months at
Moncayo.   Indeed, it was for him that I had a
very curious gun constructed . . ."

"Yes, Aranda was always opposed to it," interrupted Don Alonso, intercepting him on the dangerous ground of gunnery.

"So he did," said Don José to whom rodomontade was irresistible, "and I may say that when that distinguished man so warmly advocated peace with the republicans, it was because I advised it, being convinced from the first that the war was a mistake. But Godoy, who was then supreme, persisted in it, simply and solely to contradict me, as I have learnt since. But the best of it is that Godoy himself was obliged to put an end to the war in 1795, when he understood what it really was, and at the same time he adopted the high-sounding title of Prince of Peace."

"How much we want a good statesman, my worthy friend," said my master. "A man on a level with the times, who would not throw us into useless wars but who could maintain the dignity of the crown."

"Well, when I was at Madrid last year," continued Don José, "proposals were made to me to accept the post of Secretary of State. The Queen was most anxious for it — the King said nothing. I went with him every day to the Prado to fire a few shots. —Even Godoy would have agreed, recognizing my superior qualifications ; and indeed, if he had not I should have had no difficulty in finding some snug little fortress where I might lock him up so that he might give me no trouble. However, I declined, preferring to live in peace in my own country-town ; I left the management of public affairs in Godoy's hands. There you have a man whose father was a mule-boy on my father-in-law's estate in Estremadura. . . ."

" I did not know that. . . ." said Don Alonso. " Although he is a man of obscure origin I always supposed the Prince of Peace to belong to a family of good birth, whose fortune was impaired but whose ancestry was respectable."

And so the dialogue went on ; Señor Malespina uttering his falsehoods as if they were gospel, and my master listening with angelic calmness, sometimes annoyed by them, and sometimes amused at listening to such nonsense. If I remember rightly, Don José Maria took the credit of having advised Napoleon to the bold deeds of the 18th Brumaire.

Talking of these and of other matters we reached Chiclana as night overtook us, and my master, who was utterly tired and worn out by the villainous chaise, remained in the town, while the others went on, being anxious to reach Cadiz the same night. While we were at supper Malespina poured out a fresh farrago of lies, and I could see that his son heard them with pain, as if he were horrified at having for his father the most romancing liar in the world probably. We took leave of them and rested there till next day when we proceeded on our journey by daybreak, and as the road from Chiclana to Cadiz was much easier than that we had already traversed, we reached the end of our journey by about eleven o'clock in the morning, without adventure, safe in body and in excellent spirits.

CHAPTER VIII.

I CANNOT describe the enthusiasm that fired my mind at the sight of Cadiz. As soon as I had a moment to myself — as soon, that is to say, as my master was fairly settled in his cousin's house— I went out into the streets and ran to and fro without any fixed destination, intoxicated as it were by the atmosphere of my beloved native city. After so long an absence all I saw attracted my attention as though it were something new and beautiful. In how many of the passers-by did I recognize a familiar face ? everything charmed me and appealed to my feelings — men, women, old folks, children — the dogs, nay the houses even ; for my youthful imagination discovered in each a personal and living individuality; I felt towards them as towards intelligent creatures ; they seemed to me to express, like all else, their satisfaction at seeing me, and to wear, in their balconies and windows, the expression of gay and cheerful faces. In short my spirit saw its own gladness reflected in every surrounding object.

I hurried through the streets with eager curiosity, as if I wanted to see them all at once. In the Plaza San Juan I bought a handful of sweet-meats, less for the satisfaction of eating them than for that of introducing myself under a new aspect to the sellers, whom I addressed as an old friend ; some of them with gratitude as having been kind to me in my former misery and others as victims, not yet indemnified, to my childish pro-pensity for pillage. Most of them did not remem-ber me ; some, however, received me with abusive language, bringing up the deeds of my youth against me and making ironical remarks on my new fit-out and the dignity of my appearance, re-ducing me to flight as quickly as possible and damaging my appearance by pelting me with the rind or husks of fruit, flung by skilful hands at my new clothes. However, as I was fully convinced of my own importance, these insults increased my pride more than they hurt my feelings.

Then I went to the ramparts, and counted all the ships at anchor within sight. I spoke to sev-eral sailors that I met, telling them that I too was about to join the fleet, and asking them with eager emphasis whether they had seen Nelson's fleet; and then I assured them that *Monsieur Corneta* was no better than a coward and that the impending fight would be a grand affair. At last I reached the

creek and there my delight knew no bounds. I
went down to the shore and, taking off my shoes,
I leaped from rock to rock; I sought out my old
comrades of both sexes but I found only a few,
some who were now men had taken to some better mode of living, others had been impressed into
the ships, and those who were left hardly recognized me. The undulating motion of the water
excited my very senses; I could not resist the
temptation — urged by the mysterious spell of the
sea whose eloquent murmurs have always sounded
to me — I know not why — like a voice inviting
me to happiness or calling me with imperious
threats to rave and storm. I stripped myself as
quick as thought and threw myself into the
water as if I were flying to the arms of a lover. I
swam about for more than an hour, happy beyond
all words, and then, having dressed myself, I continued my walk to the purlieus of *la Viñá* where,
in the taverns, I came across some of the most
famous rascals of my young days. In talking with
them I gave myself out to be a man of position,
and as such, I wasted the few *cuartos* I possessed
in treating them. I asked after my uncle but no one
could give me any news of that gentleman, and
after we had chatted for awhile they made me
drink a glass of brandy which instantly went to my

head and lay me prone on the floor. During the crisis of my intoxication I thought the scoundrels were laughing at me to their hearts' content; but as soon as I recovered a little I sneaked out of the tavern much ashamed of myself. I still had some difficulty in walking; I had to go by my own old home and there, at the door, I saw a coarse-looking woman frying blood and tripe. Much touched by recognizing the home of my childhood I could not help bursting into tears and the heartless woman, seeing this, took it for granted it was some jest or trick to enable me to steal her unsavory mess. However, I was able to take to my heels and so escape her clutches, postponing the expression of my emotion till a more favorable opportunity.

After this I thought I should like to see the old Cathedral, with which the tenderest memory of my childhood was inseparably linked, and I went into it; the interior seemed to me most beautiful; never have I felt a deeper impulse of religious veneration in any church. It gave me a passionate desire to pray, and I did in fact throw myself on my knees, before the very altar where my mother had offered an *ex-voto* for my escape from death. The waxen image which I believed to be an exact likeness of myself was still

in its place which it filled with all the solemnity of
sanctity, but it struck me as very like a chestnut-
husk.   And yet this trumpery doll, the symbol of
piety and maternal devotion, filled me with tender
respect.   I said my prayers on my knees, in
memory of my good mother's sufferings and death,
and trying to realize that she was now happy in
Heaven ; but as my head was not yet very clear
of the fumes of that accursed brandy, I stumbled
and fell as I rose from my knees and an indignant
sacristan turned me out into the street.   A few
steps took me back to the Calle del Fideo,
where we were staying, and my master scolded
me for being so long absent.   If Doña Francisca
had been cognizant of my fault I should not have
escaped a sound drubbing, but my master was
merciful and never beat me, perhaps because his
conscience told him he was as much a child as I
was.

We were staying at Cadiz in the house of a
cousin of my master; and the reader must allow
me to describe this lady somewhat fully, for she
was a character deserving to be studied.   Doña
Flora de Cisniega was an old woman who still pre-
tended to be young.   She was certainly past fifty,
but she practised every art that might deceive
the world into believing her not more than half

that terrible age As to describing how she contrived to ally science and art to attain her object—
that would be an undertaking far beyond my
slender powers. The enumeration of the curls
and plaits, bows and ends, powders, rouges, washes
and other extraneous matters which she employed
in effecting this monumental work of restoration,
would exhaust the most vivid fancy; such things
may be left to the indefatigable pen of the novel-
ist — this, being History, deals only with great
subjects and cannot meddle with those elegant
mysteries. As far as her appearance was concerned what I remember best was the composition
of her face, which all the painters of the Academy
seemed to have touched up with rose color; I remember too that when she spoke she moved her
lips with a grimace, a mincing prudery which was
intended either to diminish the width of a very
wide mouth, or to conceal the gaps in her teeth
from whose ranks one or two proved deserters
every year; but this elaborate attempt was so far
a failure that it made her uglier rather than better
looking. She was always richly drest, with pounds
of powder in her hair, and as she was plump and
fair — to judge from what was visible through her
open tucker, or under the transparency of gauze
and muslin — her best chance lay in the display of

such charms as are least exposed to the injurious inroads of time, an art in which she certainly was marvellously successful.

Doña Flora was devoted to everything anti- quated, and much addicted to piety, but not with the genuine devoutness of Doña Francisca; in- deed she was in everything diametrically the oppo- site of my mistress; for while Doña Francisca hated even the glory that was won at sea, she was an enthusiastic admirer of all fighting-men and of the navy in particular. Fired by patriotic passion— since at her mature age she could not hope to feel the flame of any other — and intensely proud of herself as a woman and as a Spaniard, love of her country was symbolized in her mind by the roar of cannon, and she thought the greatness of a nation was measured by tons of gunpowder. Hav- ing no children her time was spent in gossip, picked up and passed round in a small circle of neighbors by two or three chatterboxes like her- self; but she also amused herself by her indefati- gable mania for discussing public affairs. At that time there were no newspapers, and political theories, like public news, were passed on from mouth to mouth, these being even more falsified then than now, in proportion as talk is less trust- worthy even than print.

In all the large towns, and particularly in Cadiz, which was one of the foremost cities of Spain, there were a number of idle persons who made it their business always to have the latest news from Madrid and Paris, and to be diligent in distributing it, priding themselves, in fact, on a mission which gained them so much consideration. Some of these newsmongers would meet in the evening at Doña Flora's house, and this, seconded by excellent chocolate and still better cakes, attracted others eager to learn what was going on. Doña Flora, knowing that she could not hope to inspire a tender feeling or be quit of the burthen of her fifty years, would not have exchanged the part she was thus enabled to play for any other that could have been offered to her ; for, at that time, to be the centre to which all news was conveyed was almost as precious a distinction as the majesty of a throne. Doña Flora and Doña Francisca could never get on together, as may easily be supposed when we consider the enthusiastic military tastes of one, and the pacific timidity of the other. Thus, speaking to Don Alonso the day we arrived, the good lady said :

" If you had always listened to your wife you might have been a common sailor to this day. What a woman ! If I were a man and married to

such a wife I should burst up like a bomb-shell.
You did very rightly not to follow her advice but
to come to join the fleet. Why you are not an old
man yet, Alonsito; you may still rise to the rank
of commodore, which you would have been sure
of if Paca had not clipped your wings, as we do
to chickens to prevent their straying."

When, presently, my master's eager curiosity
made him press her for the latest news, she went
on:

"The most important news is that all the naval
men here are extremely dissatisfied with the French
Admiral, who displayed his incapacity in the expedition to Martinique and the fight off Finisterre.
He is so timid and so mortally afraid of the English
that, when the combined fleets ran in here last
August, he dared not seize the cruisers commanded
by Collingwood though they were but three ships
in all. All our officers are greatly disgusted at
finding themselves obliged to serve under such a
man; indeed Gravina went to Madrid to tell
Godoy so, foreseeing some terrible disaster if the
command were not placed in more able hands;
but the minister gave him some vague answer as
to why he could not venture to decide in the matter, and as Buonaparte is in Germany, dealing with
the Austrians, he cannot be appealed to. — But it

is said that he too is dissatisfied with Villeneuve and
has determined to dismiss him ; but meanwhile. . .
If only Napoleon would put the whole fleet under
the command of some Spaniard—you, for instance,
Alonso — promoting you at once as I am sure
you richly deserve. . . ."

"Oh ! I am not fit for it!" replied my master,
with his habitual modesty.

" Well, to Gravina, or to Churruca, who is said
to be a very first-rate sailor. If not I am afraid
mischief will come of it. You cannot see the
French from here ; only think, when Villeneuve's
ships arrived they were short of victuals and ammunition, and the authorities here did not care to
supply them out of the arsenal. They forwarded
a complaint to Madrid, and as Godoy's one idea is
to do what the French ambassador M. de Bernou-
ville asks him, he sent orders that our allies should
have as much of everything as they required. But
this had no effect. The commandant of the navy
yard and the commissary of the ordnance stores
declared they would deliver nothing to Villeneuve
till he paid for it money down and in hard cash.
This seems to me very right and fair. The last
misfortune that could come upon us was that these
fine gentlemen should take possession of the little
we had left! Pretty times we live in ! Everything

is ruinously dear, and yellow fever on one side and hard times on the other had brought Andalusia to such a state that she was not worth a doit — and now, to that you add all the miseries of war. Of course the honor of the nation is the first thing and we must go on now to avenge the insults we have received. I do not want to go back to the fight of Finisterre where, through the meanness of our allies, we lost the *Firme* and the *Rafael*, two splendid ships — nor of the piratical seizure of the *Real Cárlos*, which was such an act of treachery that the Barbary pirates would have been disgraced by it — nor of the plunder of the four frigates — nor of the battle off Cape St. . . ."

"That was the thing," interrupted my master eagerly. "Every man must keep his own place, but if Admiral Córdova had given the word to tack. . . ."

"Yes, yes—I know," exclaimed Doña Flora, who had heard the story a hundred times before. "We must positively give them a thorough beating and we will. You, I know, are going to cover yourself with glory. It will enfuriate Paca."

"I am of no use for fighting," said my master sadly. "I am only going to look on, for sheer love of it and devotion to the Spanish flag."

The day after our arrival my master received

a visit from a naval officer, an old friend of his, whose face I can never forget though I saw him but that once. He was a man of about five and forty, with a really beautiful and gentle face and an expression of such tender melancholy that to see him was to love him. He wore no wig, but his abundant hair, untortured by the barber into the fashionable *ailes de pigeon*, was carelessly tied into a thick pigtail and heavily powdered, though with less elaborate care than was usual at that time. His eyes were large and blue, his nose finely chiselled, perfect in outline, rather wide, but not so wide as to disfigure him — on the contrary, it seemed to give distinction to his expressive countenance. His chin, which was carefully shaved, was somewhat pointed, and added to the melancholy charm of an oval face which was indicative of delicate feeling rather than of energetic determination. This noble exterior was well matched by the elegance of his manners — a grave courtesy of which the fatuous airs of the men of the present day retain no trace, any more than the modish graces of our *jeunesse dorée*. His figure was small, slight and even sickly looking. He looked more like a scholar than a warrior, and a brow, behind which lofty and subtle thoughts must have lain hid, looked ill-fitted to defy the horrors of battle.

7 *

His fragile form, inhabited by a soul so far above the common, looked as though it must succumb to the first shock. And yet — as I afterwards learnt — this man's heart was as brave as his intellect was supreme. It was Churruca.

Our hero's uniform, though it was not in holes nor threadbare, bore the marks of long and honorable service; afterwards, when I heard it authoritatively stated that the Government owed him nine quarters' pay, I could account for this dilapidated appearance. My master asked after his wife, and I gathered from the answer that he was only lately married, which filled me with pity; it seemed to me so terrible a thing to be dragged off to battle in the midst of so much happiness. Then they talked of his ship, the *San Juan Nepomuceno,* which he seemed to love as much as his young wife; for, as was well known, he had had it planned and fitted to his own taste, under a special privilege, and had made it one of the finest ships in the Spanish fleet. Then of course they discussed the absorbing subject of the day: whether the squadrons would or would not put out to sea and the Commodore expressed his opinion at much length, in very much such words as these; for their substance had always remained in my memory so that now, by the help of dates and historical records, I can reconstruct his speech with considerable accuracy.

"The French admiral," said Churruca, "not knowing what course to pursue and being anxious to do something which might cast his errors into oblivion, has, ever since we arrived, manifested an inclination to go and seek the English. On the 8th of October he wrote to Gravina, saying that he wished to hold a council of war on board the *Bucentaure* (Villeneuve's ship) to agree on the best course of action. Gravina went to the council, taking with him the Vice-Admiral Alava, Rear-Admirals Escaño and Cisneros, Commodore Galiano and myself. Of the French there were present Rear-Admirals Dumanoir and Magon and Captains Cosmas, Maistral, Villiegries, and Prigmy.

"Villeneuve having expressed his wish to go out to sea, we Spaniards unanimously opposed it. The discussion was warm and eager, and Alcalá Galiano and Magon exchanged such hard words that it must have come to a duel if we had not intervened to pacify them. Our opposition greatly annoyed Villeneuve, and in the heat of argument he even threw out certain insolent hints to which Gravina promptly retorted. — And indeed these worthies display a curious anxiety to go forth to seek a powerful foe, considering that they forsook us at the battle off Cape Finisterre, depriving us of what would have been a victory if they had seconded us in time. But there are many reasons, which I fully explained to the council — such as the advanced season, which render it far more advantageous for us to remain in the bay, forcing them to form a blockade which they cannot maintain, particularly if at the same time they blockade Toulon and Cartagena. We cannot but admit the superiority of the English navy, as to the completeness of their armament, their ample supply of ammunition, and, above all, the unanimity with which they manœuvre.

"We—manned for the most part with less experienced crews, inadequately armed and provided, and commanded by a leader who dissatisfies everyone — might nevertheless act to advantage on the defensive, inside the bay. But we shall be forced to obey, to succumb to the blind submission of the ministry at Madrid and put our vessels and men at the mercy of Buonaparte, who, in return for this servility has certainly not given us a chief worthy of so much sacrifice. We must go if Villeneuve orders it; but if the result is a disaster our opposition to his insane resolution stands on record as our acquittal. Villeneuve in fact is desperate; his sovereign has used harsh language to him, and the warning that he will be degraded from his command is prompting him to the maddest acts, in the hope of recovering his tarnished reputation, in a single day, by death or victory."

So spoke my master's friend. His words impressed me deeply; child as I still was, I took an eager interest in the events going on around me, and since—reading in history all the facts to which I was then witness, I have been able to aid my memory by authenticated dates so that I can tell my story with considerable accuracy.

When Churruca left us, Doña Flora and my master sang his praises in the warmest terms; praising him especially for the expedition he had conducted to Central America to make charts of those seas. According to them Churruca's merits as a navigator and a man of learning were such that Napoleon himself had made him a magnificent present and heaped civilities upon him. But we will leave the sailor and return to Doña Flora.

By the end of the second day of our stay in her house I became aware of a phenomenon which disgusted me beyond measure, which was that my master's cousin seemed quite to fall in love with me; that is to say, that she took it into her head that I was made to be her page. She never ceased to load me with every sort of kindness, and on hearing that I too was to join the fleet she bewailed herself greatly, swearing that it would be a pity if I should lose an arm or a leg, or even some less important part of my person — even if I escaped with my life. Such unpatriotic pity roused my indignation, and I believe I even went so far as to declare, in so many words, that I was on fire with warlike ardor. My gasconade delighted the old lady and she gave me a heap of sweetmeats to recover her place in my good graces.

The next day she made me clean her parrot's cage — a most shrewd bird that talked like a preacher and woke us at all hours of the morning by shrieking *"perro inglés!"*—(dog of an Englishman.) Then she took me to mass with her, desiring me to carry her stool, and in church she was incessantly looking round to see if I were there. Afterwards she kept me to look on while her hair was dressed — an operation that filled me with dismay as I saw the catafalque of curls and puffs that the hair-dresser piled on her head. Observing the stupid astonishment with which I watched the skilful manipulation of this artist — a perfect architect of head-pieces — Doña Flora laughed very heartily, and assured me that I should do better to remain with her as her page than to join the fleet, adding that I ought to learn to dress her hair, and by acquiring the·higher branches of the art I might earn my living and make a figure in the world. Such a prospect, however, had nothing seductive to my fancy, and I told her, somewhat roughly, that I would rather be a soldier than a hair-dresser. This pleased her mightily and as I was giving up the comb for something more patriotic and military she was more affectionate than ever. But notwithstanding that I was treated here with so much indulgence, I must confess that the lady annoyed me beyond measure, and that I really preferred the angry cuffing and slapping of Doña Francisca to Doña Flora's mawkish attentions. This was very natural; for her ill-timed caresses, her prudery, the persistency with which she invited my presence, declaring that she was delighted with me and my conversation, prevented my going with my master on his visits to the different ships. A servant of the house accompanied him on these delightful expeditions, while I, deprived of the liberty to run about Cadiz as I longed to be doing, was left at home, sick of life, in the society of Doña Flora's parrot and of the gentlemen who came every evening to announce whether or no the fleets would quit the bay, with other matters less to the purpose and far more trivial.

My·vexation rose to desperation when I saw
Marcial come to the house, and he and my master
went out together, though not to embark finally;
and when, after seeing them start, my forlorn
spirit lost the last faint hope of being one of the
party, Doña Flora took it into her head that she
must have me to walk with her to the Alameda
and then to church to attend vespers. This was
more than I could bear and I began to dream of
the possibility of putting a bold scheme into exe-
cution; of going, namely, on my own account to
see one of the ships, hoping that, on the quay, I
might meet some sailor of my acquaintance who
would be persuaded to take me.

I went out with the old lady and as we went
along the ramparts I tried to linger to look at the
ships, but I could not abandon myself to the enjoyment of the spectacle for I had to answer the
hundred questions with which Doña Flora per-
sistently persecuted me. In the course of our
walk we were joined by some young men and a
few older ones. They all seemed very conceited,
and were the most fashionable men of Cadiz, all
extremely witty and elegantly dressed. Some of
them were poets, or — to be accurate — wrote
verses though sorry ones, and I fancied I heard
them talking of some Academy where they met to

fire shots at each other in rhyme, an amusement which could break no bones.

As I observed all that was going on round me, their extraordinary appearance fixed my attention — their effeminate gestures and, above all, their clothes, which to me looked preposterous. There were not many persons who dressed in this style in Cadiz; and, reflecting afterwards on the difference between their costume and the ordinary clothes of the people I was in the habit of seeing, I understood that it was that men in general wore the Spanish habit while Doña Flora's friends followed the fashions of Madrid or of Paris. The first thing to attract my attention were their walking-sticks, which were twisted and knotted cudgels, with enormous knobs. Their chins were invisible, being hidden by the cravat, a kind of shawl wrapped round and round the throat and brought across below the lips so as to form a protuberance — a basket, a dish, or, better still, a barber's basin — in which the chin was quite lost. Their hair was dressed with elaborate disorder, looking as if it had been done with a birch-broom rather than with a comb. The corners of their hats came down to their shoulders; their coats, extremely short-waisted, almost swept the ground with their skirts; their boots were pointed at the toes; dozens of seals and trinkets hung from their waistcoat pockets; their breeches, which were striped, were fastened at the knee with a wide ribbon, and to put the finishing stroke to these figures of fun, each carried an eye-glass which, in the course of conversation, was constantly applied to the right eye, half-closing the left, though they would have seen perfectly well by using both.

The conversation of these gentlemen, also, turned on the plans of the fleet, but they varied it by discussing some ball or entertainment which they talked of a great deal, and one of them was the object of the greatest admiration for the perfection with which he cut capers, and the lightness of his heels in dancing the gavotte.

After chattering for some time the whole party followed Doña Flora into the church *del Cármen*, and there, each one pulling out a rosary, they remained praying with much energy for some little time, and one of them, I remember, gave me a smart rap on the top of my head because, instead of attending devoutly to my prayers like them, I was paying too much attention to two flies that were buzzing round the topmost curl of Doña Flora's structure of hair. After listening to a tiresome sermon, which they praised as a magnificent oration, we went out again, and resumed our promenade; the chat was soon more lively than ever; for we were joined by some other ladies dressed in the same style and among them all there was such a noisy hubbub of compliments, fine speeches, and witticisms, with here and there an insipid epigram, that I could gather nothing from it all.

And all this time Marcial and my dear master were arranging the day and hour when they should embark! While I was perhaps doomed to remain on shore to gratify the whims of this old woman whom I positively loathed, with her odious petting! Would you believe that that very evening she insisted on it that I must remain forever in her service? Would you believe that she declared that she was very fond of me, and in proof of the fact kissed me and fondled me, desiring me to be sure to tell no one? Horrible spite of fate! I could not help thinking what my feelings would have been if my young mistress had treated me in such a fashion. I was confused to the last degree; however, I told her that I wished to join the fleet, and that when I came back she might keep me if it was her fancy, but that if she did not allow me to have my wish I should hate her as much as that — and I spread

my arms out wide to express the immensity of
my aversion.

Then, as my master came in unexpectedly, I
thought it a favorable opportunity for gaining my
purpose by a sudden stroke of oratory which I
had hastily prepared; I fell on my knees at his
feet, declaring in pathetic accents, that if he did
not take me on board with him I should fling myself into the sea in despair.

My master laughed at this performance and
his cousin, pursing her lips, affected amusement
with a grimace which made her sallow wrinkled
face uglier than ever; but, finally, she consented.
She gave me a heap of sweetmeats to eat on
board, charged me to keep out of the way of danger, and did not say another word against my em-
barking, as we did very early next morning.

CHAPTER IX.

It was the 18th of October. I can have no doubt as to the date because the fleet sailed out of the bay next day. We rose very early and went down to the quay, where a boat was waiting to carry us on board.

Imagine if you can my surprise — nay surprise do I say? — my enthusiasm, my rapture, when I found myself on board the *Santísima Trinidad*, the largest vessel on the main, that floating fortress of timber which, seen from a distance, had appeared to my fancy some portentous and supernatural creature; such a monster as alone was worthy of the majesty of the seas. Each time our boat passed under the side of a ship I examined it with a sort of religious astonishment, wondering to see the hulls so huge that from the ramparts had looked so small; and in the wild enthusiasm that possessed me I ran the greatest danger of falling into the water as I gazed in ecstasy at a figurehead — an object which fascinated me more than anything else.

At last we reached the *Santísima Trinidad.*

As we approached, the colossal mass loomed larger and larger, and when the launch pulled up alongside, lost in the black transparent void made where its vast shadow fell upon the water — when I saw the huge hulk lying motionless on the dark waves which gently plashed against the side — when I looked up and saw the three tiers of cannon with their threatening muzzles thrust through the portholes — my excitement was changed to fear; I turned pale and sat silent and motionless by my master's side.

But when we went up the side and stood on deck my spirits rose. The intricate and lofty rigging, the busy scene on the quarter-deck, the open view of the sky and bay, the perfect order of everything on deck, from the hammocks lashed in a row to the bulwarks, to the capstans, shells, windsails and hatchways; the variety of uniforms— everything I saw, in short, amazed me to such a degree that for some time I stood blankly gazing at the stupendous structure heedless of all else. You can form no idea of any of those magnificent vessels, much less of the *Santísima Trinidad*, from the wretched prints I have seen of them. Still less, again, from the ships of war of the present day, covered with ponderous plates of iron, heavy looking, uninteresting and black, with no visible details on their vast sides, looking to me for all the world like enormous floating coffins. Invented by a materialistic age and calculated to suit the naval science of a time when steam has superseded manual labor, and the issue of a sea-fight is decided by the force and impetus of the vessels, our ships are now mere fighting-machines, while those of that day were literally Men-of-War, wielding all the implements of attack and defence but trusting mainly to skill and valor.

I, who not only see, but observe, have always been in the habit of associating — perhaps to an extravagant extent — ideas and images, things and persons, which in appearance seem most dissimilar or antagonistic. When, at a later period, I saw the cathedrals — Gothic, as they call them — of Castile and of Flanders, and noted the impressive majesty with which those perfect and elaborate structures stand up among the buildings of more modern style, built only for utility—such as banks, hospitals, and barracks — I could never help remembering all the various kinds of vessels that I have seen in the course of a long life, and comparing the old ones to those Gothic cathedrals. Their curves, so gracefully prolonged, the predominance of vertical over horizontal lines, a certain indefinable poetry about them — not historical only but religious too — underlying the complication of details and the play of colors brought out by the caprices of the sunshine, are, no doubt, what led to this far-fetched association of ideas — the result in my mind of the romantic impressions of my childhood.

The *Santísima Trinidad* had four decks; the largest ships in the World had but three. This giant, constructed at Havana, in 1769, of the finest woods of Cuba, could reckon thirty-six years of honorable service. She measured 220 feet from stem to stern, 58 feet in the waist, that is to say in width, and 28 feet deep from the keel to the deck, measurements which no other vessel at the time could approach. Her huge ribs, which were a perfect forest, supported four decks. When she was first built 116 port-holes gaped in her sides which were thick walls of timber; after she was enlarged in 1796 she had 130, and when she was newly fitted in 1805 she was made to carry 140 guns, cannons and carronades. The interior was a marvel of arrangement; there were decks for the guns, the forecastle for the crew, holds for stores of all kinds, state-cabins for the officers, the galley, the cock-pit and other offices. I was quite bewildered as I ran through the passages and endless nooks of this floating fortress. The stern cabins on the main deck were a little palace within, and outside like some fantastic castle; the galleries, the flag-turrets at the corners of the poop — exactly like the oriels of a Gothic tower—looked like huge cages open to the sea, whence the eye could command three quarters of the horizon.

Nothing could be grander than the rigging — those gigantic masts thrust up to heaven like a menace to the storm. It was difficult to believe that the wind could have strength enough to fill those vast sails. The eye lost its way and became weary in gazing at the maze of the rigging with the shrouds, stays, braces, halyards, and other ropes used to haul and reef the various sails.

I was standing lost in the contemplation of all these wonders when I felt a heavy hand on the nape of my neck; I thought the main-mast had fallen on the top of me. I turned round in alarm and gave a cry of horror at seeing a man who was now holding me by the ears as if he were going to lift me up by them. It was my uncle.

"What are you doing here, Vermin!" he asked, in the amiable tone that was habitual with him. "Do you want to learn the service? Hark ye Juan," he added, turning to a sailor of most sinister aspect, "send this landlubber up to the mainyard to take a walk there."

8 *

I excused myself as best I might from the pleasure of taking a walk on the main-yard, explaining that I was body-servant to Don Alonso Gutierrez de Cisniega and had come on board with him. Three or four sailors, my affectionate uncle's particular friends, wanted to torment me so I decided on quitting their distinguished society and went off to the cabin in search of my master. An officer's toilet is no less elaborate on board than on shore, and when I saw the valets busied in powdering the heads of the heroes they waited on, I could not help asking myself whether this was not, of all occupations, the least appropriate in a man-of-war, when every minute was precious and where everything that was not directly serviceable to the working of the ship was a hindrance. However, fashion was as tyrannical then as now, and even at such a moment as this enforced her absurd and inconvenient rules with inexorable rigor. The private soldiers even had to waste their valuable time in tying their pigtails, poor men! I saw them standing in a line, one behind another, each one at work on the pigtail of the man in front of him; by which ingenious device the operation was got through in a short space of time. Then they stuck on their fur hats, a ponderous head-piece the use of which no one was ever able to explain to me, and went to their posts if they were on duty or to pace the deck if they were not. The sailors did not wear this ridiculous queue of hair and I do not see that their very sensible costume has been altered to any great extent since that time.

In the cabin I found my master eagerly conversing with the captain in command of the ship, Don Francisco Xavier de Uriarte, and the commander of the squadron, Don Baltasar Hidalgo de Cisneros. From what I overheard I could have no doubt that the French admiral had ordered the fleets to put out to sea the next morning.

Marcial was highly delighted at this, and he and a knot of veteran sailors who held council on their own account in the forecastle, discoursed grandiloquently on the imminent fight. Their society suited me far better than that of my amiable uncle, for Marcial's companions indulged in no horse-play at my expense; and this difference was of itself enough to mark the difference of training in the two classes of sailors; for the old sea-dogs were of the pure breed originally levied as voluntary recruits; while the others were pressed men, almost without exception lazy, refractory, of low habits, and ignorant of the service.

I made much better friends with the former

than with these and was always present at Marcial's conferences.   If I did not fear to weary the
reader, I might report the explanation he gave us
that day of the diplomatical and political causes of
the war — a most comical parody of all he had
heard said, a few nights previously, by Malespina
at my master's house.   I learnt from him that
my young mistress' lover was on board the
Nepomuceno.

All these colloquies came round at last to the
same point, the impending battle.   The fleet was
to sail out of the bay next morning — what joy!
To ride the seas in this immense vessel — the
largest in the world; to witness a fight at sea; to
see what a battle was like, how cannon were fired,
how the enemy's ships were taken — what a
splendid triumph! and then to return to Cadiz
covered with glory.— To say afterwards to all
who cared to hear: "Yes, I was there, I was on
board, I saw it all...."   To tell Rosita too,
describing the glorious scene, winning her attention, her curiosity, her interest. — To say to her:
"Oh yes!   I was in the most dangerous places
and I was not afraid;" — and to see her turn
pale with alarm, or faint, as she heard my tale of
the horrors of the battle — and then to look down
in contempt on all who would ask me: "Tell us,

Gabrielito, was it so terrible after all ?" — All this was more than enough to fire my imagination, and I may frankly say that I would not, that day, have changed places with Nelson himself.

The morning of the 19th dawned, the day I hailed so eagerly ; indeed it had not yet dawned when I found myself at the stern of the vessel with my master, who wanted to look on at the working of the ship. After clearing the decks the business of starting the ship began. The huge topsails were hoisted, and the heavy windlass, turning with a shrill clatter, dragged the anchor up from the bottom of the bay. The sailors clambered along the yards, while others handled the braces, obedient to the boatswain's call ; and all the ship's voices, hitherto mute, filled the air with threatening outcries. The whistles, the bell, the discordant medley of men's voices, mixed with the creaking of the blocks, the humming of the ropes, the flapping of the sails as they thrashed the mast before they caught the wind — all these various sounds filled the air as the huge ship got under way. The bright ripples seemed to caress her sides, and the majestic monster made her way out of the bay without the slightest roll or even lurch, with a slow and solemn advance which was only perceptible to those on board by watching the apparent motion of the merchantmen lying at anchor and the landscape beyond.

At this moment I stood looking back at the scene behind us. And what a scene it was! Thirty-two men-of-war, five frigates, and two brigantines, Spanish and French together — some in front, some behind, and some abreast of us — were bursting into sail, as it were, and riding before the light breeze. I never saw a lovelier morning. The sun flooded those lovely shores with light; a faint purple tinge colored the sea to the east, and the chain of hills which bound the horizon on the side of the town seemed to be on fire in the sunrise; the sky was perfectly clear excepting where, in the east, a few rose and golden clouds floated above the horizon. The blue sea was calm, and over that sea and beneath that sky the forty ships with their white sails rode forward, one of the noblest fleets that human eyes ever rested on.

The vessels did not all sail with equal speed. Some got ahead, others were slow to get under way; some gained upon us, while we passed others. The solemnity of their advance, the height of their masts, covered with canvas, and a vague and obscure harmony which my childish ears fancied they could detect proceeding from those glorious hulls—

a kind of hymn, which was no doubt the effect of
my own imagination — the loveliness of the day,
the crispness of the air, the beauty of the sea,
which seemed to be dancing with joy outside the
gulf at the approach of the vessels — all formed
the grandest picture that the mind of man can
conceive of.

Cadiz, itself, like a moving panorama, unfolded
itself before our eyes, displaying in turn every aspect of its vast amphitheatre. The low sun, il-
luminating the glass in its myriad windows,
sprinkled it with living sparks of gold, and its
buildings lay so purely white above the blue
water that it looked as if it might have been that
moment called into being, or raised from the sea
like the fanciful city of San Genaro. I could see
the wall extending from the mole as far as the fort
of Santa Catalina; I could distinguish the bastions
of Bonete and Orejon, and recognize the *Caleta;*
and my pride rose as I reflected what I had risen
from and where I now was. At the same time the
sound of the bells of the waking city came to my
ear like some mysterious music, calling the inhabitants to early mass, with all the confused
clamor of the bells of a large town. Now they
seemed to me to ring gladly, and send good wishes
after us — I listened to them as if they were human

voices bidding us God-speed; then again they tolled sadly and dolefully — a knell of misfortune; and as we sailed further and further away their music grew fainter till it was lost in space.

The fleet slowly made its way out of the bay— some of the ships taking several hours in getting fairly to sea. Marcial meanwhile made his comments on each, watching their behavior, laughing them to scorn if they were clumsy, and encouraging them with paternal advice if they were swift and well-handled.

"What a lump that Don Federico is!" he exclaimed as he looked at the *Príncipe de Asturias* commanded by Gravina. "There goes *Mr. Corneta!*" he exclaimed as he saw the *Bucentaure* with Villeneuve on board. "He was a clever man that called you the *Rayo!*" (Thunderbolt) he cried ironically, as he watched the ship so named, which was the least manageable of all the fleet. "Well done *Papá Ignacio!*" he added, pointing to the *Santa Ana* commanded by Alava.

"Hoist your topsail properly, senseless oaf!" he went on, addressing Dumanoir's ship, *Le Formidable*. "That Frenchman keeps a hair-dresser to crimp the topsail and to clew up the sails with curling tongs!"

Towards evening the sky clouded over, and as

night fell we could see Cadiz, already at a great distance, gradually vanish in the mist till the last faint outline became one with the darkness. The fleet then steered to the Southward.

All night I kept close to Marcial, as soon as I had seen my master comfortably settled in his cabin. The old sailor, eagerly listened to by a couple of veteran comrades and admirers, was explaining Villeneuve's plan of battle.

"*Mr. Corneta*," said he, "has divided the fleet into four lines. The vanguard led by Alava consists of six vessels; the centre, likewise of six, is commanded by *Mr. Corneta* in person; the rear, again of six, is under Dumanoir, and the reserve of twelve ships is led by Don Federico. This seems to me not badly planned. I imagine that the French and Spanish ships are mixed, in order that they may not leave us impaled on the bull's horns as they did at Finisterre.

"From what Don Alfonso tells me the Frenchman says that if the enemy comes up to leeward we are to form in line of battle and attack at once. . . . This is very pretty talk in the stateroom; but do you think the *Señorito* will be such a booby as to come up to leeward of us? Oh yes — his lordship has not much brains in his figure-head and is sure to let himself be caught in that trap! Well! we shall see — if we see, what the Frenchman expects! — If the enemy gets to windward and attacks us we are to receive him in line of battle, and as he must divide to attack if he does not succeed in breaking our line, it will be quite easy to beat him. Everything is easy to *Mr. Corneta* (applause). He says too that he shall give no signals, but expects every captain to do his best. If we should see what I have always prophesied, ever since that accursed subsidy treaty, and that is — but I had better hold my tongue.— Please God....! Well I have always told you that Mr. Corneta does not understand the weapons he has in his hands; there is not room in his head for fifty ships. What can you think of an admiral, who, the day before a battle, sends for his captains and tells each of them to do what he thinks will win the day. — After that! (Strong expressions of sympathy). However, we shall see what we shall see. — But do you just tell me: If we Spanish want to scuttle a few of those English ships, are we not strong enough and many enough to do it? Then why in the world need we ally ourselves with the French, who would not allow us to do anything we had a mind to, but would have us dancing attendance at the end of their tow-line? Whenever we have had to work with them they have got us into mischief and we have had the worst of it. Well — may God and the Holy Virgin *del Cármen* be on our side, and rid us of our French friends for ever and ever, Amen." (Great Applause.)

All his audience agreed heartily ; the discussion was continued till a late hour, rising from the details of naval warfare to the science of diplomacy. The night was fine and we ran before a fresh breeze — I must be allowed to say " *We*" in speaking of the fleet. I was so proud of finding myself on board the *Santísima Trinidad* that I began to fancy that I was called to play some important part on this great occasion, and I could not forbear from swaggering about among the sailors to let them see that I was not there for nothing.

CHAPTER X.

ON the morning of the 20th there was a stiff breeze blowing and the vessels kept at some distance from each other; but as the wind had moderated soon after noon the admiral signalled that the ships were to form in five lines — the van, centre, and rear, and two lines of reserve. I was enchanted with watching the docile monsters, obediently taking their places; for, although the conditions of naval manœuvres did not admit of great rapidity nor of perfect uniformity in the line, it was impossible to see them without admiration. The wind was from the southwest, according to Marcial, and the fleet, catching the breeze on the starboard quarter, ran towards the straits. During the night a few lights were seen and by dawn on the 21st we saw twenty-seven ships to windward, among which Marcial pointed out three as three-deckers. By eight o'clock the thirty-three vessels of the enemy's fleet were in sight, forming two columns. Our fleet displayed a wide front, and to all appearance Nelson's two columns, advancing in a wedge, were coming down upon us so as to cut our lines through the centre and rear.

This was the position of the hostile fleets when the *Bucentaure* signalled that we were to put about; maybe you do not understand this. It means that we were to turn completely round and that whereas the wind was on our port side it would now be on the starboard, so that we should sail in the opposite direction. The ships' heads were now turned northwards and this manœuvre, which was intended to place us to windward of Cadiz so that we might reach it in case of disaster, was severely criticised on board the *Trinidad*, especially by Marcial, who said:

"The line of battle is all broken up; it was bad before and is worse now."

In point of fact what had been the vanguard was now in the rear and the reserve ships, which as I heard said, were the best, were hindmost of all. The wind had fallen and the ships, being of various tonnage and inefficiently manned, the new line could not form with due precision; some of the vessels moved quickly and rushed forward; others went slowly, hanging back or losing their course, and forming a wide gap that broke the line before the enemy took the trouble of doing it.

"Reform the line" was now the signal; but, though a good ship answers her helm with wonderful docility, it is not so easy to manage as a horse. As he stood watching the movements of the ships nearest to us, Marcial observed: "The line is wider than the milky-way. If the *Señorito* cuts through it, Heaven help us! we shall not be able to sail in any sort of order; they will shave our heads for us if they fire upon us. They are going to give us a dose through the centre and how can the *San Juan* and the *Bahama* come up to support us from the rear — or the *Neptuno* and the *Rayo* which are in front. (Murmurs of applause.) Besides, here we are to leeward and the 'great-coats' can pick and choose where they will attack us, while all we can do is to defend ourselves as best we may. All I have to say is: God get us well out of the scrape and deliver us from the French for ever and ever, Amen."

The sun had now nearly reached the meridian and the enemy was coming down upon us.

"And is this a proper hour to begin a battle?" asked the old sailor indignantly. "Twelve o'clock in the day!"

But he did not dare to express his views publicly and these discussions were confined to a small circle into which I, with my eternal and in-

satiable curiosity, had squeezed myself. I do not
know why, but it seemed to me that there was an
expression of dissatisfaction on every face. The
officers on the quarter-deck, and the sailors and
non-commissioned officers at the bows, stood
watching the ships to leeward, quite out of the
line of battle, four of which ought to have been in
the centre.

I forgot to mention one preliminary in which
I myself had borne a hand. Early in the morning the decks were cleared for action, and when
all was ready for serving the guns and working
the ship, I heard some one say: "The sand —
bring the sand." Marcial pulled me by the ear,
and taking me to one of the hatchways set me in
a line with some of the pressed men, ship's boys,
and other supernumeraries. A number of sailors
were posted on the ladders from the hatchway to
the hold and between decks, and in this way were
hauling up sacks of sand. Each man handed one
to the man next to him and so it was passed on
without much labor. A great quantity of sacks
were thus brought up from hand to hand, and to
my great astonishment they were emptied out on
the upper deck, the poop, and the forecastle, the
sand being spread about so as to cover all the
planking; and the same thing was done between

decks. My curiosity prompted me to ask the boy who stood next to me what this was for.

" For the blood," he said very coolly.

" For the blood !" I exclaimed unable to repress a shudder. I looked at the sand — I looked at the men who were busily employed at this task — and for a moment I felt I was a coward. However, my imagination reverted to the ideas which had previously filled it, and relieved my mind of its alarms; I thought no more of anything but victory and a happy issue.

Everything was ready for serving the guns and the ammunition was passed up from the store-rooms to the decks by a chain of men, like that which had brought up the sand-bags.

The English advanced to attack us in two sections. One came straight down upon us, and at its head, which was the point of the wedge, sailed a large ship carrying the admiral's flag. This, as I afterwards learned, was the *Victory*, commanded by Nelson. At the head of the other line was the *Royal Sovereign*, commanded by Collingwood. All these names, and the strategical plan of the battle, were not known to me till later.

My recollections, which are vividly distinct as to all the graphic and picturesque details, fail me with regard to the scheme of action which was beyond my comprehension at the time. All that I picked from Marcial, combined with what I subsequently learnt, sufficed to give me a good idea of the arrangement of our fleets; and for the better intelligence of the reader I give in the next page a list of our ships, indicating the gaps left by those that had not come up, and the nationality of each.

It was now a quarter to twelve. The fatal moment was approaching. The anxiety was general, and I do not speak merely from what was going on in my own mind, for I was absorbed in watching the ship which was said to contain Nelson, and for some time was hardly aware of what was going on round me.

Suddenly a terrible order was given by our captain — the boatswains repeated it; the sailors flew to the tops; the blocks and ropes creaked, the topsails flapped in the wind.

"Take in sail!" cried Marcial, with a good round oath. "The infernal idiot is making us work back."

And then I understood that the *Trinidad* was to slacken her speed so as to run alongside of the *Bucentaure*, because the *Victory* seemed to be taking measures to run in between those two ships and so cut the line in the middle.

Neptuno,   Sp....... ⎫
Le Scipion, Fr....... ⎪
Rayo, Sp............. ⎪
Le Formidable, Fr...... ⎬ Front.
——Le Duguay Trouin, Fr. ⎪
Le Mont Blanc, Fr....... ⎪
Asís,   Sp................ ⎭

San Augustin, Sp.......... ⎫
Le Héros, Fr.............. ⎪
Victory   Trinidad, Sp................. ⎪
Nelson.   Le Bucentaure, Fr........... ⎬ Centre.
——————>——— Neptune, Fr............. ⎪
Le Redoutable,· Fr............. ⎪
L'Intrépide, Fr................. ⎪
——— Leandro, Sp............... ⎭

Royal
Sovereign   ———Justo, Sp.................... ⎫
Collingwood. ——— L'Indomptable, Fr........... ⎬
—————> Santa Ana, Sp.................... ⎪ Rear.
Le Fougueux, Fr.................. ⎪
Monarca, Sp....................... ⎪
Le Pluton, Fr..................... ⎭

Bahama, Sp........................... ⎫
——— L'Aigle, Fr...................... ⎪
Montañes, Sp......................... ⎪
Algeciras, Sp........................ ⎪
Argonauta, Sp........................ ⎪
Swiftsure, Fr........................ ⎪
——— L'Argonaute, Fr.................. ⎬ Reserve.
Ildefonso, Sp........................ ⎪
——— L'Achille, Fr.................... ⎪
Príncipe de Astúrias, Sp................. ⎪
Le Berwick, Fr....................... ⎪
Nepomuceno, Sp. :.................... ⎭

In watching the working of our vessel I could see that a great many of the crew had not that nimble ease which is usually characteristic of sailors who, like Marcial, are familiar with war and tempests. Among the soldiers several were suffering from sea-sickness and were clinging to the ropes to save themselves from falling. There were among them many brave souls, especially among the volunteers, but for the most part they were impressed men, obeying orders with an ill-will and not feeling, I am very sure, the smallest impulse of patriotism. As I afterwards learnt, nothing but the battle itself made them worthy to fight. In spite of the wide differences in the moral stamp of all these men, I believe that during the solemn moments that immediately preceded the first shot a thought of God came to every mortal there.

So far as I am concerned, in all my life my soul has never gone through any experiences, to compare with those of that hour. In spite of my youth, I was quite capable of understanding the gravity of the occasion, and for the first time in my life, my mind was filled with grand ideas, lofty aspirations and heroic thoughts. A conviction that we must conquer was so firmly rooted in my mind that I felt quite pitiful towards the English, and wondered to see them so eagerly advancing to certain destruction. For the first time too I fully understood the ideal of patriotism, and my heart responded to the thought with a glow of feeling such as I had never experienced before. Until now my mother-country had been embodied in my mind in the persons of its rulers—such as the King and his famous minister, for whom I felt different degrees of respect. As I knew no more of history than I had picked up in the streets, it was to me a matter of course that everybody's enthusiasm must be fired by knowing that the Spaniards had, once upon a time, killed a great number of Moors, and, since then, swarms of French and of English. I considered my countrymen as models of valor; but valor, as I conceived of it, was as like barbarity as one egg is like another; and with such ideas as these, patriotism had been to me nothing more than boastful pride in belonging to a race of exterminators of Moors.

But in the pause that preceded the battle I understood the full significance of that divine word; the conception of nationality, of devotion to a mother-country, was suddenly born in my soul, lighting it up, as it were, and revealing a thousand wonderful possibilities — as the rising sun dissipates the darkness that has hidden a beautiful landscape. I thought of my native land as a vast place full of people all united in brotherly regard — of society as divided into families, married couples to be held together, and children to be educated—of honor, to be cherished and defended; I imagined an unspoken agreement among all these human beings to help and protect each other against any attack from without, and I understood that these vessels had been constructed by them all for the defence of their native land; that is to say, for the soil on which they lived, the fields watered by their sweat, the homes where their ancestors had dwelt, the gardens where their children played, the colonies discovered and conquered by their forefathers, the harbors where their ships found shelter after long voyages — the magazines where they stored their wealth—the Church which was the mausoleum of those they had loved, the dwelling-place of their saints, and the ark of their belief— the public places where they might take their pleasure, the private homes where the venerable household gods, handed down from generation to generation, seemed to symbolize the perpetuity of the nation—their family hearth round which the smoke-dyed walls seem still to re-echo with the time-honored legends with which the grand dame soothes the flightiness or the naughtiness of the

little ones, the street where friendly faces meet
and smile — the field, the sea, the sky — everything which from the moment of birth makes up
the sum of existence, from the crib of a pet animal
to the time-honored throne of the king; every object into which the soul seems to go forth to live,
as if the body that clothes it were too narrow a
shell.

I believed too that the disputes between Spain
and France or England were always about something that those countries ought to give up to us,
and in which Spain could not, on the whole, be
wrong. Her self-defence seemed to me as legiti-
mate as the aggression was brutal; and as I had
always heard that justice must triumph, I never
doubted of victory. Looking up at our red and
yellow flag — the colors nearest to that of fire —
I felt my bosom swell, and could not restrain a
few tears of enthusiasm and excitement; I thought
of Cadiz, of Vejer, of the whole Spanish nation
assembled, as it were, on a vast platform and
looking on with eager anxiety; and all this tide
of emotion lifted up my heart to God to whom I
put up a prayer, which was neither a *Paternoster*
nor an *Ave*, but a gush of inspiration that came
to me at the moment.

A sudden shock startled me from my ecstasy,

terrifying me with its violent vibration. The first broadside had been fired.

CHAPTER XI.

A VESSEL in the rear had been the first to fire on the *Royal Sovereign*, commanded by Collingwood, and while that ship carried on the fight with the *Santa Ana* the *Victory* came down on us. On board the *Trinidad* every one was anxious to open fire; but our captain would not give the word till he saw a favorable opportunity. Meanwhile, as if the ships were in such close communication that a slow-match was lighted from one to the other, the fire ran along from the *Santa Ana* in the middle, to each end of the line.

The *Victory* fired first on the *Redoutable*, and being repulsed, came up to the windward of the *Trinidad*. The moment had come for us; a hundred voices cried "fire!"—loudly echoing the word of command, and fifty round-shot were hurled against the flank of the English man-of-war. For a minute I could see nothing of the enemy for the smoke, while he, as if blind with

rage, came straight down upon us before the wind.
Just within gun-shot he put the ship about and
gave us a broadside.   In the interval between our
firing and theirs, our crew, who had taken note of
the damage done to the enemy, had gained in
enthusiasm.   The guns were rapidly served,
though not without some hitches owing to want
of experience in some of the gunners.   Marcial
would have been only too glad to undertake the
management of one of the cannon, but his mutilated body was not equal to the heroism of his
spirit.   He was forced to be satisfied with super-
intending the delivery of the charges and encouraging the gunners by word and gesture.

The *Bucentaure*, just at our stern, was, like us,
firing on the *Victory* and the *Téméraire*, another
powerful English vessel.   It seemed as though
the *Victory* must fall into our hands, for the *Trinidad's* fire had cut her tackle to pieces, and we saw
with pride that her mizzen-mast had gone by the
board.

In the excitement of this first onslaught I
scarcely perceived that some of our men were
wounded or killed.   I had chosen a place where
I thought I should be least in the way, and never
took my eyes off the captain who stood on the
quarter-deck, issuing his orders with heroic cool-

ness; and I wondered to see my master, no less
calm though less enthusiastic, encouraging the
officers and men in his quavering voice.

"Ah!" said I to myself, "if only Doña Francisca could see him now!"

I am bound to confess that at times I felt
desperately frightened, and would gladly have
hidden myself at the very bottom of the hold,
while, at others, I was filled with an almost deli-
rious courage, when I longed to see the glorious
spectacle from the most dangerous posts. However, I will set aside my own insignificant individuality and relate the most terrible crisis of our
fight with the *Victory*. The *Trinidad* was doing
her immense mischief when the *Téméraire*, by a
wonderfully clever manœuvre, slipped in between
the two vessels thus sheltering her consort from
our fire. She then proceeded to cut through the
line behind the *Trinidad*, and as the *Bucentaure*,
under fire, had got so close alongside of the *Trinidad* that their yards touched, there was a wide
space beyond into which the *Téméraire* rushed
down and, going about immediately, came up on
our lee and delivered a broadside on that quarter,
till then untouched. At the same time the *Neptune*, another large English ship, ran in where the
Victory had previously been, while the *Victory*

veered round so that, in a few minutes, the *Trinidad* was surrounded by the enemy and riddled on all sides.

From my master's face, from Uriarte's heroic fury, and from a volley of oaths delivered by Marcial and his friends, I understood that we were lost and the idea of defeat was anguish to my soul. The line of the combined fleets was broken at several points, and the bad order in which they had formed after turning round, gave place to the most disastrous confusion. We were surrounded by the enemy whose artillery kept up a perfect hail of round and grape-shot on our ship, and on the *Bucentaure* as well. The *Agustin*, the *Héros*, and the *Leandro* were engaged at some distance from us where they had rather more sea-room, while the *Trinidad*, and the Admiral's ship, utterly hemmed in and driven to extremities by the genius of the great Nelson, were fighting heroically — no longer in hopes of a victory which was impossible but anxious, at any rate, to perish gloriously.

The white hairs which now cover my old head almost stand on end as I remember those terrible hours, from two to four in the afternoon. I think of those five ships, not as mere machines of war obeying the will of man, but as living giants, huge,

creatures fighting on their own account, carried
into action by their sails as though they were active limbs and using the fearful artillery they bore
in their sides for their personal defence. As I
looked at them then, my fancy could not help per-
sonifying them and to this hour I feel as though I
could see them coming up, defying each other,
going about to fire a broadside, rushing furiously
up to board, drawing back to gather more force,
mocking or threatening the enemy;—I can
fancy them expressing their suffering when
wounded or loftily breathing their last, like a
gladiator who in his agony forgets not the dignity
which beseems him;—I can imagine that I hear
the voices of the crews like the murmur of an
oppressed sufferer, sometimes eager with enthusiasm, sometimes a dull roar of desperation the
precursor of destruction, sometimes a hymn of
triumph in anticipation of victory, or a hideous
storm of voices lost in space and giving way to
the awful silence of disgrace and defeat.

The scene on board the *Santísima Trinidad*
was nothing short of infernal. All attempt at
working the ship had been abandoned, for it did
not and could not move. The only thing to be
done was to serve the guns with the utmost
.rapidity, and to do as much damage to the enemy

as they had done to us. The English small-shot rent the sails just as if huge and invisible nails were tearing slits in them. The splinters of timber and of masts, the stout cables cut through as if they were straws, the capstans, spindles, and other heavy machinery torn from their place by the enemy's fire, strewed the deck so that there was scarcely room to move. Every minute men, till then full of life, fell on deck or into the sea; the blasphemy of those who were fighting mingled with the cries of the wounded, till it was impossible to say whether the dying were defying God or the living crying to him for mercy while they fought.

I offered my services for a melancholy task, which was carrying the wounded into the cockpit where the surgeons were busy doing their utmost. Some were dead before we could get them there, and others had to suffer painful operations before their exhausted bodies could be left to repose.

Then I had the extreme satisfaction of helping the carpenters who were constantly employed in repairing the holes made in the ship's sides; but my youth and inefficiency made me less useful than I would fain have been.

Blood was flowing in rivulets on the upper and

lower decks and in spite of the sand the motion of the ship carried it from side to side making sinister patterns on the boards. The canon-balls, fired at such a short range, mutilated those they killed in a terrible manner, and I saw more than one man still standing with his head blown away, the force of the shock not having been great enough to fling the victim into the sea, whose waters would have extinguished almost painlessly the last sensation of existence. Other balls struck a mast or against the bulwarks, carrying off a hail of hot splinters that pierced and stung like arrows. The rifle-shots from the tops and the round-shot from the carronades dealt a more lingering and painful death, and there was hardly a man to be seen who did not bear the marks, more or less severe, of the foe's iron and lead.

The crew — the soul of the ship — being thus thrashed by the storm of battle and utterly unable to deal equal destruction, saw death at hand though resolved to die with the courage of despair; and the ship itself — the glorious body — shivered under the cannonade. I could feel her shudder under the fearful blows; her timbers cracked, her beams creaked, her ribs groaned like limbs on the rack, and the deck trembled under my feet with audible throbs, as though the whole huge creature was indignant at the sufferings of her crew. Meanwhile the water was pouring in at a hundred holes in the riddled hull, and the hold was fast filling.

The *Bucentaure*, the Admiral's vessel, surrendered before our very eyes. Villeneuve struck to the *Victory*. When once the leader of the fleet was gone, what hope was there for the other ships? The French flag vanished from the gallant vessel's mast and she ceased firing. The *San Augustin* and the *Héros* still persevered, and the *Rayo* and *Neptuno*, of the van, made an effort to rescue us from the enemy that was battering us. I could see what was going on in the immediate neighborhood of the *Trinidad*, though nothing was to be seen of the rest of the line. The wind had fallen to a calm and the smoke settled down over our heads shrouding everything in its dense white wreaths which it was impossible for eye to pierce. We could catch a glimpse now and then of a distant ship, mysteriously magnified by some inexplicable optical effect; I believe indeed that the terror of that supreme moment exaggerated every impression.

Presently this dense cloud was dispersed for an instant — but in what a fearful manner! A tremendous explosion, louder than all the thousand guns of the fleet fired at once, paralyzed every man and filled every soul with dread; and just as the ear was stunned by the terrific roar an intense flash lighted up the two fleets, rending the veil of smoke and revealing the whole panorama of the battle. This catastrophe had taken place on the side towards the South where the rear line had been posted.

"A ship blown up!" said one to another. But opinion differed as to whether it was the *Santa Ana*, the *Argonauta*, the *Ildefonso*, or the *Bahama*. We afterwards learnt that it was a Frenchman, the *Achille*. The explosion scattered in a myriad fragments what had a few moments before been a noble ship of 74 guns and 600 men. But a few seconds after we had already forgotten the explosion in thinking only of ourselves.

The *Bucentaure* having struck, the enemy's fire was directed on us, and our fate was sealed. The enthusiasm of the first hour was by this extinct in my soul; my heart quaked with terror that paralyzed my limbs and smothered every other emotion excepting curiosity. This I found so irresistible that I could not keep away from places where the danger was greatest. My small assistance was of no great use now, for the wounded were too numerous to be carried below and the guns had to be served by those who had some little strength left. Among these was Marcial who was here, there, and everywhere, shouting and working to the best of his small ability, acting as boatswain, gunner, sailor, and carpenter all at once, doing everything that happened to be needed at this awful moment. No one could have believed that, with hardly more than half a body, he could have done the work of so many men. A splinter had struck him on the head and the blood had stained his face and given him a most horrible appearance. I could see his lips move as he licked the blood from them and then he spit it out viciously over the side, as if he thought he could thus punish the enemy.

What astonished me most, and indeed shocked me somewhat, was that Marcial even in this scene of horror could still cut a good-humored joke; whether to encourage his dejected comrades or only to keep his own courage up I do not know. The foremast fell with a tremendous crash, covering the whole of the fore-deck with rigging, and Marcial called out to me: "Bring the hatchets, boy; we must stow this lumber in Davy Jones' locker," and in two minutes the ropes were cut and the mast went overboard.

Then, seeing that the enemy's fire grew hotter, he shouted to the purser's mate, who had come up to serve a gun: "Daddy, order up some drink for those ' great-coats,' and then they will let us alone."

To a soldier, who was lying like a dead creature with the pain of his wounds and the misery of sea-sickness, he exclaimed as he whisked the slow-match under his nose: " Take a whiff of orange-flower, man, to cure your faintness. Would you like to take a turn in a boat ? Nelson has invited us to take a glass of grog with him."

This took place amidships ; looking up at the quarter-deck I saw that Cisneros was killed ; two sailors hastily carried him down into his cabin. My master remained immovable at his post, but his left arm was bleeding severely.   I ran up to help him, but before I could reach the spot an officer had gone to him to persuade him to retire to his state-room.   He had not spoken two words when a ball shot away half his head and his blood sprinkled my face.   Don Alonso withdrew, as pale as the corpse which fell on the quarter-deck. When my master had gone down the commander was left standing alone, so perfectly cool that I could not help gazing at him for a few minutes, astounded by such courage.   His head was uncovered, his face very white, but his eyes flashed

and his attitude was full of energy, and he stood
at his post, commanding the desperate strife,
though the battle was lost past retrieval. Even
this fearful disaster must be conducted with due
order, and the captain's duty was still to keep discipline over heroism. His voice still controlled
his men in this struggle between honor and death.
An officer who was serving in the first battery
came up for orders, and before he could speak he
was lying dead at the feet of his chief; another
officer of marines who was standing by his side
fell wounded on the deck, and at last Uriarte
stood quite alone on the quarter-deck, which was
strewn with the dead and wounded. Even then
he never took his eyes off the English ships and
the working of our guns—the horrible scene on
the poop and in the round-house, where his comrades and subalterns lay dying, could not quell his
noble spirit nor shake his firm determination to
face the fire till he too should fall. As I recall the
fortitude and stoical calmness of Don Francisco
Xavier de Uriarte, I understand all that is told us
of the heroes of antiquity. At that time the word
Sublime was as yet unknown to me, but I felt that
there must be, in every language under heaven,
some human utterance to express that greatness
of soul which I here saw incarnate and which re-

vealed itself to me as a special grace vouchsafed by God to miserable humanity.

By this time most of our guns were silenced, more than half of our men being incapable of serving them. I might not, however, have been aware of the fact, but that being impelled by curiosity I went out of the cabin once more and heard a voice saying in a tone of thunder:

"Gabrielillo, come here."

It was Marcial who was calling me; I ran to his side and found him trying to work one of the guns which had been left silent for lack of men. A ball had shot away the half of his wooden leg, which made him exclaim: "Well! so long as I can manage to keep the one of flesh and bone. . . . !"

Two sailors lay dead by the gun; a third, though horribly wounded, still tried to go on working it.

"Let be, mate!" said Marcial. "You cannot even light the match," and taking the linstock from his hand, he put it into mine, saying: "Take it, Gabrielillo.—If you are afraid you had better jump overboard."

He loaded the cannon as quickly as he was able, helped by a ship's boy who happened to come up;

we ran it forward: "fire!" was the word, I applied the match and the gun went off.

We repeated this operation a second and a third time, and the roar of the cannon fired by my own hand produced an extraordinary effect on my nerves. The feeling that I was no longer a spectator but an actor in this stupendous tragedy for the moment blew all my alarms to the winds; I was eager and excited, or at any rate determined to appear so. That moment revealed to me the truth that heroism is often simply the pride of honor. Marcial's eye—the eyes of the world were upon me; I must bear myself worthy of their gaze.

"Oh!" I exclaimed to myself with an impulse of pride: "If only my young mistress could see me now!... Bravely firing cannon like a man!" Two dozen of English were the least I might have sent to the other world.

These grand visions, however, did not last long for Marcial, enfeebled by age, was beginning to sink with exhaustion; he breathed hard as he wiped away the blood which flowed profusely from his head, and at last his arms dropped by his side, and closing his eyes, he exclaimed: "I can do no more; the powder is rising to my head. Gabrielillo, fetch me some water."

I ran to obey him, and when I had brought
the water he drank it eagerly. This seemed to give
him fresh energy ; we were just about to load once
more when a tremendous shock petrified us as we
stood.   The main-mast, cut through by repeated
shots, fell amidships and across the mizzen ; the
ship was completely covered with the wreck, and
the confusion was appalling.

I happily was so far under shelter that I got no
harm but a slight blow on the head which, though
it stunned me for a moment, did not prevent my
thrusting aside the fragments of rope and timber
which had fallen above me. The sailors and marines
were struggling to clear away the vast mass of
lumber, but from this moment only the lower-deck
guns could be used at all.   I got clear as best I
could and went to look for Marcial but I did not
find him, and casting my eyes up at the quarter-
deck, I saw that the captain was no longer at his
post.   He had fallen senseless, badly wounded in
the head by a splinter, and two sailors were just
about to carry him down to the state-room.   I was
running forward to assist when a piece of shell hit
me on the shoulder, terrifying me excessively, for
I made sure my wound was mortal and that I was
at my last gasp. My alarm did not hinder me from
going into the cabin ; I tottered from loss of blood

and for a few minutes lay in a dead faint. I was roused from my short swoon by hearing the rattle of the cannon below and then a voice shouting vehemently:

"Board her! bring pikes! — axes!"

And then the confusion was so complete that it was impossible to distinguish human voices from the rest of the hideous uproar. However, some-how — I know not how — without thoroughly waking from my drowsy state, I became aware that all was given up for lost and that the officers had met in the cabin to agree to strike; nor was this the work of my fancy, bewildered as I was, for I heard a voice exclaiming: "The *Trinidad* never strikes!" I felt sure that it was Marcial's voice; but at any rate some one said it.

When I recovered perfect consciousness, I saw my master sunk on one of the sofas in the cabin, his face hidden in his hands, prostrate with despair, and paying no heed to his wound.

I went to the heart-broken old man, who could find no way of expressing his grief but by embrac-ing me like a father, as if we were both together on the brink of the grave. He, at any rate, was con-vinced that he must soon die of grief, though his wound was by no means serious. I comforted him as best I might, assuring him that if the battle were indeed lost it was not because I had failed to batter the English to the best of my power; and I went on to say that we should be more fortunate next time — but my childish arguments failed to soothe him.

Going out presently in search of water for my master, I witnessed the very act of lowering the flag which was flying at the gaff, that being one of the few spars, with the remains of the mizzen-mast, that remained standing. The glorious flag, the emblem of our honor, pierced and tattered as it was, which had gathered so many fighting-men under its folds, ran down the rope never to be unfurled again. The idea of stricken pride, of a brave spirit giving way before a superior force, can find no more appropriate symbol to represent it than that of a flying standard which sinks and disappears like a setting sun. And our flag thus slowly descending that fatal evening, at the moment when we surrendered, seem to shed a parting ray of glory.

The firing ceased, and the English took possession of the conquered vessel.

CHAPTER XII.

WHEN. the mind had sufficiently recovered from the shock and excitement of battle, and had time to turn from " the pity of it " and the chill of terror left by the sight of that terrific struggle, those who were left alive could see the hapless vessel in all its majesty of horror. Till now we had thought of nothing but self-defence, but when the firing ceased we could turn our attention to the dilapidated state of the ship, which let in the water at a hundred leaks and was beginning to sink, threatening to bury us all, living and dead, at the bottom of the sea. The English had scarcely taken possession when a shout arose from our sailors, as from one man :

" To the pumps !"

All who were able flew to the pumps and labored hard at them; but these ineffectual machines turned out much less water than poured in. Suddenly a shriek even more appalling than any we had heard before filled us with horror. I have said that the wounded had been carried down into the hold which, being below the water line, was secure from the inroads of the cannon shot. But the water was fast gaining there, and some sailors came scrambling up the hatchways exclaiming that the wounded were being drowned. The greater part of the crew hesitated between continuing to pump and running down to rescue the hapless wretches; and God knows what would have happened if an English crew had not come to our assistance. They not only carried up the wounded to the second and third deck but they lent a hand at the pumps and their carpenters set to work to stop the leaks in the ship's sides.

Utterly tired out, and thinking too that Don Alonso might need my services, I returned to the cabin. As I went I saw some Englishmen hoisting the English flag at the bows of the *Trinidad*. As I dare to believe that the amiable reader will allow me to record my feelings, I may say that this incident gave me something to think of. I had always thought of the English as pirates or sea-highwaymen, as a race of adventurers not worthy to be called a nation but living by robbery. When I saw the pride with which they hauled up their flag, saluting it with vociferous cheering; when I perceived the satisfaction it was to them to have made a prize of the largest vessel that, until then, had ever sailed the seas, it struck

me that their country, too, was dear to them, that
her honor was in their hands and I understood
that in that land — to me so mysteriously remote
— called England, there must be, as in Spain,
honorable men, a paternal king, mothers, daugh-
ters, wives, and sisters of these brave mariners —
all watching anxiously for their return and praying to God for victory.

I found my master in the cabin, somewhat
calmer.   The English officers who had come on
board treated ours with the most distinguished
courtesy and, as I heard, were anxious to transfer
the wounded on board their own ship.   One of
these gentlemen went up to my master as if
recognizing him, bowed to him, and addressing
him in fairly-good Spanish, reminded him of an
old acquaintanceship.   Don Alonso responded
gravely to his advances and then enquired of him
as to some of the details of the battle.

"But what became of our reserve?   What
did Gravina do?" asked my master.

"Gravina withdrew with some of his ships,"
replied the English officer.

"Only the *Rayo* and *Neptuno* came to our
assistance of all the front line?"

"Four French ships — the *Duguay-Trouin*,

the *Mont Blanc*, the *Scipion*, and the *Formidable* were the only ones that kept out of the action."

"But Gravina — where was Gravina?" Don Alonso persisted.

"He got off in the *Príncipe de Astúrias;* but as he was chased I do not know whether he reached Cadiz in safety."

"And the *San Ildefonso?*"

"She struck."

"And the *Santa Ana?*"

"Struck too."

"Good God!" cried my master, unable to conceal his indignation. "But you did not take the *Nepomuceno?*"

"Yes, that too."

"Are you sure of that? With Churruca?"

"He was killed," said the Englishman with sincere regret.

"Killed — Churruca killed!" exclaimed Don Alonso in grievous bewilderment. "And the *Bahama* — she was saved — the *Bahama* must have been able to reach Cadiz in safety."

"She was taken too."

"Taken! And Galiano? He is a hero and a cultivated gentleman."

"He was," said the Englishman sadly, "but he too is dead."

" And the *Montañés* with Alcedo ?"

" Killed, killed."

My master could not control his emotion and as, at his advanced age, presence of mind is lacking at such terrible moments, he suffered the slight humiliation of shedding a few tears as he remembered his lost friends. Nor are tears unbecoming to a noble soul ; on the contrary, they reveal a happy infusion of delicate feeling, when combined with a resolute temper. My master's tears were manly tears, shed after he had done his duty as a sailor ; but, hastily recovering from this paroxysm of grief, and anxious to retort on the Englishman by some pain equal to that he had caused, he said :

" You too have suffered, no doubt, and have lost some men of mark ? "

" We have suffered one irreparable loss," said the English officer in accents as deeply sad as Don Alonso's. " We have lost our greatest man, the bravest of the brave — our noble, heroic, incomparable Nelson."

And his fortitude holding out no better than my master's he made no attempt to conceal his anguish of grief; he covered his face with his hands and wept with the pathetic frankness of incontrollable sorrow for his leader, his guardian, and his friend.

Nelson, mortally wounded at an early stage of the battle by a gun-shot — the ball piercing his chest and lodging in the spine — had simply said to Captain Hardy: "They have done for me at last, Hardy." He lingered till the evening, not losing any details of the battle, and his naval and military genius only failed him with the last breath of his shattered body. Though suffering agonies of pain, he still dictated his orders and kept himself informed of the manœuvres of both fleets; and when at length he was assured that victory was on the side of the English, he exclaimed: "Thank God, I have done my duty!" A quarter of an hour later the greatest sailor of the age breathed his last. The reader will forgive me this digression.

It may seem strange that we did not know the fate of many of the ships of the combined fleets. But nothing could be more natural than our ignorance, considering the great length of our front and the plan of isolated fights contrived and carried out by the English. Their vessels had got mixed up with ours and the ships fought at close quarters; the one which had engaged us hid the rest of the squadron from view, besides which

the dense smoke prevented our seeing anything
that was not quite close to us. Towards nightfall
and before the firing had altogether ceased, we
could distinguish a few ships in the offing, looking
like phantoms; some with half their rigging gone,
and others completely dismasted. The mist, the
smoke and, indeed, our own wearied and bewildered brains, would not allow us to distinguish
whether they were our own or the enemy's, and
as, from time to time the glare of a broadside in
the distance lighted up the lugubrious scene, we
could see that the fight was still going on to a
desperate end between detached groups of ships,
while others were flying before the wind without
aim or purpose, and some of ours were being
towed by the English to the South.

Night fell, increasing the misery and horror of
our situation. It might have been hoped that
Nature at least would be on our side after so much
disaster; but, on the contrary, the elements
lashed us with their fury as though Heaven
thought our cup of misfortune was not yet full.
A tremendous storm burst and the winds and
waves tossed and buffeted our ship in their fury
and, as she could not be worked, she was utterly
at their mercy. The rolling was so terrible that
it was very difficult even to work the pumps, and

this, combined with the exhausted condition of the men, made our condition grow worse every minute. An English vessel, which as we learnt was the *Prince*, tried to take us in tow; but her efforts were in vain and she was forced to keep off for fear of a collision which would have been fatal to both.   Meanwhile it was impossible to get anything to eat, and I was dying of hunger, though the others seemed insensible to anything but the immediate danger and gave no thought to this important matter.   I dared not ask for a piece of bread even, for fear of seeming greedy and troublesome; but at the same time, I must confess — and without shame — I looked out sharply to see if there were any place where I might hope to find any kind of eatable stores. Emboldened by hunger, I made free to inspect the hold where the biscuit-boxes were kept, and what was my astonishment at finding Marcial there before me, stowing himself with every thing he could lay his hands on.   The old man's wound was not serious, and though a ball had carried away his right foot, as this was only the lower end of his wooden leg the mishap only left him a little more halt than before.

"Here, Gabrielillo," he said, giving me a heap of biscuits, "take these.   No ship can sail without ballast." And then he pulled out a bottle and drank with intense satisfaction. As we went out of the biscuit-room we saw that we were not the only visitors who had made a raid upon it; on the contrary, it was very evident that it had been well pillaged not long since.

Having recruited my strength I could now think of trying to make myself useful by lending a hand at the pumps or helping the carpenters. They were laboriously repairing some of the damage done, aided by the English, who watched all our proceedings; indeed, as I have since learnt, they kept an eye on every one of our sailors, for they were afraid lest we should suddenly mutiny and turn upon them to recapture the vessel; in this, however, the enemy showed more vigilance than common-sense, for we must indeed have lost our wits before attempting to recover a ship in such a condition. However, the "great-coats" were everywhere at once, and we could not stir without being observed.

Night fell, and as I was perishing with cold I quitted the deck where I could scarcely bear myself besides incurring constant risk of being swept overboard by a wave, so I went down into the cabin. My purpose was to try to sleep a little while — but who could sleep in such a night?

The same confusion prevailed in the cabin as on deck. Those who had escaped unhurt were doing what they could to aid the wounded, and these, disturbed by the motion of the vessel which prevented their getting any rest, were so pitiable a sight that it was impossible to resign one's self to sleep. On one side, covered with the Spanish flag, lay the bodies of the officers who had been killed; and in the midst of all this misery, surrounded by so much suffering, these senseless corpses seemed really to be envied. They alone on board the *Trinidad* were at rest, to them nothing mattered now: fatigue and pain, the disgrace of defeat, or physical sufferings. The standard which served them as a glorious winding-sheet shut them out, as it were, from the world of responsibility, of dishonor, and of despair, in which we were left behind. They could not care for the danger the vessel was in, for to them it was no longer anything but a coffin.

The officers who were killed were Don Juan Cisniega, a lieutenant in the navy, who was not related to my master, in spite of their identity of name; Don Joaquin de Salas and Don Juan Matute, also lieutenants; Don José Graullé, lieutenant-colonel in the army; Urias, lieutenant in command of a frigate, and midshipman Don

11 *

Antonio de Bobadilla. The sailors and marines whose corpses lay strewn about the gun-decks and upper-deck amounted to the terrible number of four hundred.

Never shall I forget the moment when the bodies were cast into the sea, by order of the English officer in charge of the ship. The dismal ceremony took place on the morning of the 22nd when the storm seemed to be at its wildest on purpose to add to the terrors of the scene. The bodies of the officers were brought on deck, the priest said a short prayer for this was no time for elaborate ceremonial, and our melancholy task began. Each wrapped in a flag, with a cannon-ball tied to his feet, was dropped into the waves without any of the solemn and painful emotion which under ordinary circumstances would have agitated the lookers-on. Our spirits were so quelled by disaster that the contemplation of death had become almost indifference. Still, a burial at sea is more terribly sad than one on land. We cover the dead with earth and leave him there; those who loved him know that there is a spot where the dear remains are laid and can mark it with a slab, a cross, or a monument; but at sea — the body is cast into that heaving, shifting waste; it is lost forever as it disappears; imagination cannot follow it in its fall — down, down to the fathomless abyss; it is impossible to realize that it still exists at the bottom of the deep. These were my reflections as I watched the corpses vanish — the remains of those brave fighting-men, so full of life only the day before — the pride of their country and the joy of all who loved them.

The sailors were thrown overboard with less ceremony; the regulation is that they shall be tied up in their hammocks, but there was no time to carry this out. Some indeed were wrapped round as the rules require, but most of them were thrown into the sea without any shroud or ball at their feet, for the simple reason that there were not enough for all. There were four hundred of them, more or less, and merely to clear them overboard and out of sight every able-bodied man that was left had to lend a hand, so as to get it done as quickly as possible. Much to my horror I saw myself forced to offer my services in the dismal duty, and many a dead man dropped over the ship's side at a push from my hand helping other and stronger ones.

One incident — or rather coincidence — occurred which filled me with horror. A body horribly mauled and mutilated had been picked up by two sailors, and just as they lifted it one or two of the by-standers allowed themselves to utter some of those coarse and grim jests which are always offensive, and at such a moment revolting. I know not how it was that this poor wretch was the only one which moved them so completely to lose the sense of reverence due to the dead, but they exclaimed: "He has been paid out for old scores — he will never be at his tricks again," and other witticisms of the same kind. For a moment my blood rose, but my indignation suddenly turned to astonishment mingled with an indescribable feeing of awe, regret, and aversion, when, on looking at the mangled features of the corpse, I recognized my uncle. I shut my eyes with a shudder, and did not open them again till the splash of the water in my face told me that he had disappeared forever from mortal ken. This man had been very cruel to me, very cruel to his sister; still, he was my own flesh and blood, my mother's brother; the blood that flowed in my veins was his, and that secret voice which warns us to be charitable to the faults of our own kith and kin could not be silenced after what I had seen, for at the moment when I recognized him I had perceived in those blood-stained features some reminder of my mother's face, and this stirred my deepest feelings. I forgot that the man had been a brutal wretch, and all his barbarous treatment of me during my hapless childhood. I can honestly declare — and I venture to do so though it is to my own credit — that I forgave him with all my heart and lifted up my soul to God, praying for mercy on him for all his sins.

I learnt afterwards that he had behaved gallantly in the fight, but even this had not won him the respect of his comrades who, regarding him as a low sneak, never found a good word for him — not even at that supreme moment when, as a rule, every offence is forgiven on earth in the belief that the sinner is rendering an account to his Maker.

As the day advanced the *Prince* attempted once more to take the *Santísima Trinidad* in tow, but with no better success than before. Our situation was no worse, although the tempest raged with undiminished fury, for a good deal of the mischief had been patched up, and we thought that if the weather should mend the hulk, at any rate, might be saved. The English made a great point of it, for they were very anxious to take the largest man-of-war ever seen afloat into Gibraltar as a trophy; so they willingly plied the pumps by night and by day and allowed us to rest awhile. All through the day of the 22nd the sea continued terrific, tossing the huge and helpless vessel as though it were a little fishing-boat, and the enormous mass of timber proved the soundness of her build by not simply falling to pieces under the furious lashing of the waters. At some moments she rolled over so completely on her beam ends that it seemed as though she must go to the bottom, but suddenly the wave would fly off in smoke, as it were, before the hurricane, the ship, righting herself, rode over it with a toss of her mighty prow — which displayed the Lion of Castile — and we breathed once more with the hope of escaping with our lives.

On all sides we could see the scattered fleets; many of the ships were English, severely damaged and striving to gain shelter under the coast. There were Frenchmen and Spaniards too, some dismasted, others in tow of the enemy. Marcial recognized the *San Ildefonso*. Floating about were myriads of fragments and masses of wreck — spars, timbers, broken boats, hatches, bulwarks, and doors — besides two unfortunate sailors who were clinging to a plank, and who must have been swept off and drowned if the English had not hastened to rescue them. They were brought on board more dead than alive, and their resuscitation after being in the very jaws of death was like a new birth to them.

That day went by between agonies and hopes ——now we thought nothing could save the ship and that we must be taken on board an Englishman, then again we hoped to keep her afloat. The idea of being taken into Gibraltar as prisoners was intolerable, not so much to me perhaps as to men of punctilious honor and sensitive dignity like my master whose mental anguish at the thought must have been intolerable. However, all the torment of suspense, at any rate, was relieved by the evening when it was unanimously agreed that if we were not transferred to an English ship at once, to the bottom we must go with the vessel, which now had five feet of water in the hold. Uriarte and Cisneros took the announcement with dignified composure, saying that it mattered little to them whether they perished at once or were prisoners in a foreign land. The task was at once begun in the doubtful twilight, and as there were above three hundred wounded to be transferred it was no easy matter. The available number of hands was about five hundred, all that were left uninjured of the original crew of eleven hundred and fifteen before the battle.

We set to work promptly with the launches of the *Trinidad* and the *Prince*, and three other boats belonging to the English. The wounded were attended to first; but though they were lifted with all possible care they could not be moved without great suffering, and some entreated with groans and shrieks to be left in peace, preferring immediate death to anything that could aggravate and prolong their torments. But there was no time for pity, and they were carried to the boats as ruthlessly as the cold corpses of their comrades had been flung into the sea.

Uriarte and Cisneros embarked in the English captain's gig, but when they urged my master to accompany them he obstinately refused, saying that he wished to be last to leave the sinking ship. This I confess disturbed me not a little, for as by this time, the hardy patriotism which at first had given me courage had evaporated, I thought only of saving my life, and to stay on board a foundering vessel was clearly not the best means to that laudable end. Nor were my fears ill founded, for not more than half the men had been taken off when a dull roar of terror echoed through the ship.

"She is going to the bottom — the boats, to the boats!" shouted some, and there was a rush

to the ship's side, all looking out eagerly for the
return of the boats. Every attempt at work or
order was given up, the wounded were forgotten,
and several who had been brought on deck
dragged themselves to the side in a sort of deli-
rium, to seek an opening and throw themselves
into the sea. Up through the hatchways came a
hideous shriek which I think I can hear as I write,
freezing the blood in my veins and setting my
hair on end. It came from the poor wretches on
the lowest deck who already felt the waters rising
to drown them and vainly cried for help—to God
or men — who can tell ! Vainly indeed to men,
for they had enough to do to save themselves.
They jumped wildly into the boats, and this confusion in the darkness hindered progress. One
man alone, quite cool in the midst of the danger,
remained in the state cabin, paying no heed to all
that was going on around him, walking up and
down sunk in thought, as though the planks he
trod were not fast sinking into the gulf below. It
was my master. I ran to rouse him from his
stupefaction. "Sir," I cried, "we are drowning !"

Don Alonzo did not heed me, and if I may
trust my memory he merely said without looking
round :

"How Paca will laugh at me, when I go home after such a terrible defeat!"

"Sir, the ship is sinking!" I insisted, not indeed exaggerating the danger, but in vehement entreaty.

My master looked at the sea, at the boats, at the men who were blindly and desperately leaping overboard; I looked anxiously for Marcial and called him as loudly as I could shout. At the same time I seemed to lose all consciousness of where I was and what was happening. I turned giddy and I could see nothing. To tell how I was saved from death I can only trust to the vaguest recollections, like the memory of a dream, for in fact I fairly swooned with terror. A sailor, as I fancy, came up to Don Alonso while I was speaking to him; in his strong arms I felt myself lifted up and when I somewhat recovered my wits I found myself in one of the boats, propped up against my master's knees, while he held my head in his hands with fatherly care and kindness. Marcial held the tiller and the boat was crowded with men.

Looking up I saw, apparently not more than four or five yards away, the black side of our ship sinking fast; but through the port-holes of the deck that was still above water I could see a dim light—that of the lamp which had been lighted at dusk and which still kept unwearied watch over the wreck of the deserted vessel. I still could hear the groans and cries of the hapless sufferers whom it had been impossible to remove and who were within a few feet of the abyss while, by that dismal lamp they could see each other's misery and read each other's agony in their eyes.

My fancy reverted to the dreadful scene on board — another inch of water would be enough to overweight her and destroy the little buoyancy that was left her. How far did those poor creatures understand the nearness of their fate? What were they saying in this awful moment? If they could see us safe in our boat — if they could hear the splash of our oars, how bitterly must their tortured souls complain to Heaven! But such agonizing martyrdom must surely avail to purify them of all guilt, and the grace of God must fill that hapless vessel, now when it was on the point of disappearing for ever!

Our boat moved away; and still I watched the shapeless mass — though I confess that I believe it was my imagination rather than my eyes that discerned the *Trinidad* through the darkness, till I believe I saw, against the black sky, a huge arm reaching down to the tossing waters—

the effect no doubt of my imagination on my senses.

CHAPTER XIII.

THE boat moved on — but whither? Not Marcial himself knew where he was steering her to. The darkness was so complete that we lost sight of the other boats and the lights on board the *Prince* were as invisible through the fog, as though a gust of wind had extinguished them. The waves ran so high and the squalls were so violent that our frail bark made very little way, but thanks to skilful steering she only once shipped water. We all sat silent, most of us fixing a melancholy gaze on the spot where we supposed our deserted comrades were at this moment engaged in an agonizing death-struggle. In the course of this passage I could not fail to make, as was my habit, certain reflections which I may venture to call philosophical. Some may laugh at a philosopher of fourteen; but I will not heed their laughter; I will try to write down the thoughts that occupied me at this juncture. Children too can think great thoughts and at such a moment, in face of such a spectacle, what brain but an idiot's could remain unmoved.

There were both English and Spaniards in our boat—though most Spaniards—and it was strange to note how they fraternized, helping and encouraging each other in their common danger, and quite forgetting that only the day before they had been killing each other in hideous fight, more like wild beasts than men. I looked at the English who rowed with as good a will as our own sailors, I saw in their faces the same tokens of fear or of hope, and above all the same expression, sacred to humanity, of kindness and fellowship which was the common motive of all. And as I noted it I said to myself: "Good God! why are there wars? Why cannot these men be friends under all the circumstances of life as they are in danger? Is not such a scene as this enough to prove that all men are brothers?"

But the idea of nationality suddenly occurred to me to cut short these speculations, and my geographical theory of islands. "To be sure," said I to myself, "the islands must need want to rob each other of some portion of the land, and that is what spoils everything. And indeed there must be a great many bad men there who make wars for their own advantage, because they are ambitious and wish for power, or are avaricious and wish for wealth. It is these bad men who deceive the rest — all the miserable creatures who do the fighting for them; and to make the fraud complete, they set them against other nations, sow discord and foment envy — and here you see the consequences. I am certain" — added I to myself, " that this can never go on; I will bet two to one that before long the inhabitants of the different Islands will be convinced that they are committing a great folly in making such tremendous wars, and that a day will come when they will embrace each other and all agree to be like one family." So I thought then; and now, after sixty years of life, I have not seen that day dawn.

The launch labored on through the heavy sea. I believe that if only my master would have consented Marcial would have been quite ready to pitch the English overboard and steer the boat to Cadiz or the nearest coast, even at the imminent risk of foundering on the way. I fancy he had suggested something of the kind to Don Alonso, speaking in a low voice, and that my master wished to give him a lesson in honor, for I heard him say:

"We are prisoners, Marcial — we are prisoners."

The worst of it was that no vessel came in sight. The *Prince* had moved off, and no light on either side told us of the existence of an English ship. At last, however, we descried one at some distance and a few minutes later the vague outline came in sight of a ship before the storm, to our windward, and on the opposite tack to ours. Some thought it was a Frenchman, others said it was English; Marcial was sure she was a Spaniard. We pulled hard to meet her and were soon within speaking distance. Our men hailed her and the answer was in Spanish.

" It is the *San Agustin*," said Marcial.

" The *San Agustin* was sunk," said Don Alonso; " I believe it is the *Santa Ana* which was also captured." In fact, as we got close, we all recognized the *Santa Ana* which had gone into action under the command of Alava. The English officers in charge immediately prepared to take us on board, and before long we were all safe and sound on deck.

The *Santa Ana*, 112 guns, had suffered severely; though not to such an extent as the *Santísima Trinidad;* for, though she had lost all her masts and her rudder, the hull was fairly sound. The *Santa Ana* survived the battle of Trafalgar eleven years, and would have lived much

longer if she had not gone to the bottom for want
of repairs in the bay of Havana, in 1816. She
had behaved splendidly in the fight. She was
commanded, as I have said, by Vice-admiral
Alava leader of the van which, as the order of
battle was altered, became the rear. As the
reader knows, the line of English ships led by
Collingwood attacked the Spanish rear while Nelson took the centre. The *Santa Ana*, only supported by the *Fougueux*, a Frenchman, had to
fight the *Royal Sovereign* and four other English
ships; and in spite of their unequal strength one
side suffered as much as the other, for Collingwood's ship was the first to retire and the *Eury-
alus* took her place. By all accounts the fighting
was terrific, and the two great ships, whose masts
were almost entangled, fired into each other for
six hours until Alava and Gardogui, both being
wounded (Alava subsequently died), five officers
and ninety-seven sailors being killed, besides more
than 150 wounded, the *Santa Ana* was forced to
surrender. The English took possession of her,
but it was impossible to work her on account of
her shattered condition, and the dreadful storm
that rose during the night of the 21st; so when
we went on board she was in a very critical,
though not a desperate situation, floating at the

mercy of the wind and waves and unable to make any course. From that moment I was greatly comforted by seeing that every face on board betrayed a dread of approaching death. They were all very sad and quiet, enduring with a solemn mien the disgrace of defeat and the sense of being prisoners. One circumstance I could not help observing, and that was that the English officers in charge of the ship were not by a great deal so polite or so kind as those sent on board the *Trinidad ;* on the contrary, among those on the *Santa Ana* were some who were both stern and repellent, doing all they could to mortify us, exaggerating their own dignity and authority, and interfering in everything with the rudest impertinence. This greatly annoyed the captured crew, particularly the sailors ; and I fancied I overheard many alarming murmurs of rebellion which would have been highly disquieting to the English if they had come to their ears.

Beyond this there is nothing to tell of our progress that night—if progress it can be called when we were driven at the will of the wind and waves, sailless and rudderless. Nor do I wish to weary the reader with a repetition of the scenes we had witnessed on board the *Trinidad,* so I will go on

12 *

to other and newer incidents which will surprise
him as much as they did me.

I had lost my liking for hanging about the
deck and poop, and as soon as we got on board
the *Santa Ana* I took shelter in the cabin with
my master, hoping to get food and rest, both of
which I needed sorely.   However, I found there
many wounded who required constant attention
and this duty, which I gladly fulfilled, prevented
my getting the sleep which my wearied frame required.   I was engaged in placing a bandage on
Don Alonso's arm when a hand was laid on my
shoulder.   I turned round and saw a tall young
officer wrapped in a large blue cloak whom I did
not immediately recognize; but after gazing at
him for a few seconds, I exclaimed aloud with
surprise ; it was Don Rafael Malespina, my young
mistress's lover.

My master embraced him affectionately and
he sat down by us.   He had been wounded in the
shoulder, and was so pale from fatigue and loss of
blood that his face looked quite altered.   His
presence here filled me with strange sensations —
some of which I am fain to own were anything
rather than pleasing.   At first I felt glad enough
indeed to see any one I knew and who had come
out alive from those scenes of horror, but the next

moment my old aversion for this man rose up, as strong as ever in my breast, like some dormant pain reviving to torment me after an interval of respite. I confess with shame that I was sorry to see him safe and sound, but I must do myself the justice to add that the regret was but momentary, as brief as a lightning flash — a flash of blackness, as I may say, darkening my soul; or rather a transient eclipse of the light of conscience which shone clearly again in the next instant. The evil side of my nature for a moment came uppermost; but I was able to suppress it at once and drive it down again to the depths whence it had come. Can every one say as much?

After this brief mental struggle I could look at Malespina, glad that he was alive and sorry that he was hurt; and I remember, not without pride, that I did all I could to show him my feelings. Poor little mistress! How terrible must her anguish have been all this time. My heart overflowed with pitiful kindness at the thought — I could have run all the way to Vejer to say: "Señorita Doña Rosa, your Don Rafael is safe and sound."

The luckless Malespina had been brought on board the *Santa Ana* from the *Nepomuceno*, which had also been captured, and with so many wounded on board that it had been necessary, as we learnt, to distribute them or they must have perished of neglect. When the father and his daughter's *fiancé* had exchanged the first greetings and spoken of the absent ones on shore, the conversation turned on the details of the battle. My master related all that had occurred on board the *Trinidad* and then he added : " But no one has told me exactly what has become of Gravina. Was he taken prisoner, or has he got off to Cadiz ?"

" The Admiral," said Malespina, " stood a terrific fire from the *Defiance* and the *Revenge.* The *Neptune*, a Frenchman, came to her assistance with the *San Ildefonso* and the *San Justo ;* but our enemies were reinforced by the *Dreadnought*, the *Thunderer*, and the *Polyphemus* ; so that resistance was hopeless. Seeing the *Príncipe de Astúrias* with all her tackle cut, her masts overboard and her sides riddled with balls, while Gravina himself and Escaño, his second in command, were both wounded, they resolved on giving up the struggle which was quite in vain for the battle was lost. Gravina hoisted the signal to retire on the stump of a mast and sailed off for Cadiz, followed by the *San Justo*, the *San Leandro*, the *Montañes* and three others ; only regretting their inability to rescue the *San Ildefonso* which had fallen into the hands of the enemy."

"But tell us what happened on board the *Nepomuceno*," said my master, deeply interested. "I can hardly believe that Churruca can be dead; and, though every one tells me that he is, I cannot help fancying that that wonderful man must still be alive somewhere on earth."

But Malespina told him that it had been his misfortune to see Churruca killed and said he would relate every detail. A few officers gathered round him while I, as curious as they could be, was all ears in order not to lose a syllable.

"Even as we came out of Cadiz," said Malespina, "Churruca had a presentiment of disaster. He had voted against sailing out to sea, for he knew the inferiority of our armament, and he also had little confidence in Villeneuve's skill and judgment. All his predictions were verified—all, even to his own death: for there is no doubt that he had foreseen it as surely as he did our defeat. On the 19th he had said to Apodaca, his brother-in-law, before going on board: 'Sooner than surrender my ship, I will blow her up or go to the bottom. That is the duty of every man who serves his king and country.' And the same day, writing to a friend, he said: 'If you hear that my ship is taken you will know that I am dead.'

"Indeed it was legible in his sad grave face

that he looked forward to nothing but a catastrophe. I believe that this conviction, and the absolute impossibility of avoiding defeat while feeling himself strong enough for his own part, seriously weighed upon his mind, for he was as capable of great deeds as he was of noble thoughts.

"Churruca's was a religious as well as a superior mind. On the 21st., at eleven in the morning, he called up all the soldiers and crew; he bid them all kneel and said to his chaplain in solemn tones : 'Fulfil your function, holy Father, and absolve these brave souls that know not what this fight may have in store for them.' When the priest had pronounced absolution Churruca desired them to stand up, and speaking in friendly but audible tones he added :   'My children all:—In God's name I promise heavenly bliss to all who die doing their duty.   If one of you shirks it he shall be shot on the spot ; or, if he escapes my notice or that of the gallant officers I have the honor to command, his remorse shall pursue him so long as he crawls through the rest of his miserable and dishonored days.'

"This harangue, as eloquent as it was wise, combining the ideas of religion and of military duty, filled every man on board with enthusiasm. Alas for all these brave hearts !—wasted like gold sunk at the bottom of the ocean! Face to face with the English, Churruca watched Villeneuve's preliminary manœuvres with entire disapproval, and when the signal was given for the whole fleet to turn about—a manœuvre which, as we know, reversed the order of battle—he told his captain in so many words that this blunder had lost us the day. He immediately understood the masterly plan struck out by Nelson of cutting our line through the centre from the rear, and engaging the whole fleet at once, dealing with our ships in separate divisions so that they could not assist each other.

"The *Nepomuceno* was at the end of the line. The *Royal Sovereign* and the *Santa Ana* opened fire and then all the ships in turn came into action. Five English vessels under Collingwood attacked our ship; two, however, passed on and Churruca had only three to deal with.

"We held out bravely against these odds till two in the afternoon, suffering terribly, however, though we dealt double havoc on the foe. Our Admiral seemed to have infused his heroic spirit into the crew and soldiers, and the ship was handled and the broadsides delivered with terrible promptitude and accuracy. The new recruits had learnt their lesson in courage in no more than a couple of hours' apprenticeship, and our defence struck the English not merely with dismay but with astonishment.

"They were in fact forced to get assistance and bring up no less than six against one. The two ships that had at first sailed past now returned, and the *Dreadnought* came alongside of us, with not more than half a pistol-shot between her and our stern. You may imagine the fire of these six giants pouring balls and small shot into a vessel of 74 guns. But our ship seemed positively to grow bigger in proportion to the desperate bravery of her defenders. They themselves seemed to grow in strength as their courage mounted, and seeing the dismay we created in an enemy six times as strong, we could have believed ourselves something more than men.

"Churruca, meanwhile, who was the brain of us all, directed the action with gloomy calmness. Knowing that only care and skill could supply the place of strength he economized our fire, trusting entirely to careful aim, and the consequence was that each ball did terrible havoc on the foe. He saw to everything, settled everything, and the shot flew round him and over his head without his ever once changing color even. That frail and delicate man, whose beautiful and melancholy

features looked so little fitted to dare such scenes
of terror, inspired us all with unheard-of courage,
simply by a glance of his eye.

"However, it was not the will of God that he
should escape alive from that storm of fire. Seeing that no one could hit one of the enemy's
ships which was battering us with impunity, he
went down himself to judge of the line of fire and
succeeded in dismasting her. He was returning
to the quarter-deck when a cannon ball hit his
right leg with such violence as almost to take it
off, tearing it across the thigh in the most frightful manner. We rushed to support him and our
hero sank into my arms. It was a fearful moment. I still fancy I can feel his heart beating
under my hand — a heart which, even at that terrible moment, beat only for his country. He
sank rapidly. I saw him make an effort to raise
his head, which had fallen forward on his breast;
I saw him try to force a smile while his face was
as white as death, and he said, in a voice that was
scarcely weaker than usual: 'It is nothing — go
on firing.'

"His spirit revolted against death and he did
all he could to conceal the terrible sufferings of
his mutilated frame, while his heart beat more
feebly every instant. We wanted to carry him

down into the cabin, but nothing would persuade him to quit the quarter-deck. At last he yielded to our entreaties and understood that he must give up the command. He called for Moyna, his lieutenant, and was told that he was dead; then he called for the officer in command of the first battery, and the latter though himself seriously wounded at once mounted the quarter-deck and assumed the command.

"But from that moment the men lost heart; from giants they shrank to pigmies; their courage was worn out and it was plain that we must surrender. The consternation that had possessed me from the instant when our hero fell into my arms had not prevented my observing the terrible effect that this disaster had produced in the minds of all. A sudden paralysis of soul and body seemed to have fallen on the crew; they all stood petrified and speechless and the grief of losing their beloved leader quite overpowered the disgrace of surrender.

" Quite half of the men were dead or wounded; most of the guns were past serving; all the masts except the main-mast were gone by the board and the rudder could not be used. Even in this deplorable plight we made an attempt to follow the *Príncipe de Astúrias* which had given the signal to retreat, but the *Nepomuceno* was mortally wounded and could not move nor steer. Even then, in spite of the wrecked state of the ship, in spite of the dismayed condition of the men, in spite of a concurrence of circumstances to render our case hopeless, not one of the six English captains attempted to board us. They respected our ship even when she was at their mercy.

"Churruca, in the midst of his agony, ordered that the flag should be nailed to the mast, for the ship should never surrender so long as he breathed. The delay alas! could be but brief, for Churruca was going rapidly, and we who supported him only wondered that a body so mangled could still breathe; it was his indomitable spirit that kept him alive added to a resolute determination to live, for he felt it his first duty. He never lost consciousness till the very end, nor complained of his sufferings, nor seemed to dread his approaching death; his sole care and anxiety was that the crew should not know how dangerous his condition was, so that no one should fail in his duty. He desired that the men should be thanked for their heroic bravery, spoke a few words to his brother-in-law, Ruiz de Apodaca, and, after sending a message to his young wife he fixed his thoughts on God, whose name we heard fre-

quently on his parched lips, and died with the
calm resignation of a just man and the fortitude of
a hero; bereft of the satisfaction of victory but
with no angry sense of defeat.   In him duty and
dignity were equally combined, and discipline was
second only to religion.   As a soldier he was
resolute, as a man he was resigned, and without a
murmur or an accusing word he died as nobly as
he had lived.   We looked at his body, not yet
cold, and it seemed all a delusion — he must
surely wake to give us our orders; and we wept
with less fortitude than he had shown in dying, for
in him we had lost all the valor and enthusiasm
that had borne us up.

" Well, the ship struck ; and when the officers
from the six vessels that had destroyed her came
on board each claimed the honor of receiving the
sword of our dead hero.   Each exclaimed: ' He
surrendered to me !'— and for a few minutes they
eagerly disputed the victory, each for the ship he
represented.   Then they asked the officer who had
taken the command to which of the Englishmen
he had struck.   ' To all,' he replied.   ' The *Nepomuceno* would never have surrendered to one.'

" The English gazed with sincere emotion on
the body of the hapless Churruca, for the fame of
his courage and genius was known to them and

one of them spoke to this effect: 'A man of such illustrious qualities ought never to be exposed to the risks of battle ; he should be kept to live and serve the interests of science and navigation.' Then they prepared for dropping him overboard, the English marines and seamen forming a line of honor alongside of the Spaniards ; they behaved throughout like noble-minded and magnanimous gentlemen.

"The number of our wounded was very considerable, and they were transferred on board other English or captured ships. It was my lot to be sent to this one which has suffered worse than most ; however, they count more on getting her into Gibraltar than any other, now that they have lost the *Trinidad* which was the finest and most coveted of our ships."

Thus ended Malespina's narrative which was attentively listened to as being that of an eye-witness. From what I heard I understood that a tragedy just as fearful as that I myself had seen had been enacted on board every ship of the fleet. "Good God !" said I to myself, "what infinite misery ! and all brought about by the obstinacy of a single man !" And child as I was, I remember thinking : "One man, however mad he may be, can never commit such extravagant follies as

whole nations sometimes plunge into at the bidding of a hundred wise ones."

CHAPTER XIV.

A LARGE part of the night was spent in listening to Malespina's narrative and the experiences
of other officers. They were interesting enough
to keep me awake and I was so excited that I
found great difficulty afterwards in going to sleep
at all. I could not get the image of Churruca out
of my mind as I had seen him, handsome and
strong, at Doña Flora's house. On that occasion,
even, I had been startled by the expression of intense sadness on the hero's features, as if he had
a sure presentiment of his near and painful death.
His noble life had come to an untimely end when
he was only forty-four years old, after twenty-nine
years of honorable service as a soldier, a navigator,
and a man of science — for Churruca was all of
these, besides being a noble and cultivated gentlemen. I was still thinking of all these things when,
at length, my brain surrendered to fatigue and I
fell asleep on the morning of the 23rd, my youthful nature having got the better of my excitement

and curiosity. But in my sleep, which was long
if not quiet, I was still haunted by nightmare
visions, as was natural in my overwrought state of
mind, hearing the roar of cannon, the tumult of
battle and the thunder of billows; meanwhile I
fancied I was serving out ammunition, climbing
the rigging, rushing about between decks to encourage the gunners and even standing on the
quarter-deck in command of the vessel. I need
hardly say that in this curious but visionary battle
I routed all the English past, present, or to come,
with as much ease as though their ships were
made of paper and their cannon-balls were bread-
pills. I had a thousand men-of-war under my
command, each larger than the *Trinidad*, and they
moved before me with as much precision as the
toy-ships with which I and my comrades had been
wont to play in the puddles of *la Caleta*.

At last, however, all this glory faded away,
which, as it was but a dream, is scarcely to be
wondered at when we see how even the reality
vanishes. It was all over when I opened my eyes
and remembered how small a part I had actually
played in the stupendous catastrophe I had witnessed. Still — strange to say — even when wide
awake I heard cannon and the all-dreadful tumult
of war, with shouts and a clatter that told of some

great turmoil on deck. I thought I must still be
dreaming; I sat up on the sofa on which I had
fallen asleep; I listened with all my ears, and certainly a thundering shout of " God save the King"
left no doubt in my mind that the *Santa Ana* was
fighting once more.

I went out of the cabin and studied the situation. The weather had moderated; to the windward a few battered ships were in sight, and two
of them, Englishmen, had opened fire on the *Santa
Ana* which was defending herself with the aid of
two others, a Frenchman and a Spaniard. I could
not understand the sudden change in the aspect of
affairs. Were we no longer prisoners of war ? I
looked up — our flag was flying in the place of the
Union Jack. What could have happened ? — or
rather what was happening ? For the drama was
in progress.

On the quarter-deck stood a man who, I con-
cluded, must be Alava, and though suffering from
several wounds he still had strength enough to
command this second action, which seemed likely
enough to recover the honor his good ship had
lost in the disaster of the first. The officers were
encouraging the sailors who were serving those
guns that could still be worked, while a detach-
ment kept guard over the English, who had been

disarmed and shut up in the lower deck. Their officers who had been our jailers were now become our prisoners.

I understood it all. The brave commander of the *Santa Ana*, Don Ignacio de Alva, seeing that we were within hail of some Spanish ships, which had come out of Cadiz in hope of rescuing some of our captured vessels and to take off the survivors from such as might be sinking, had addressed a stirring harangue to his disheartened crew who responded to his enthusiasm by a supreme effort. By a sudden rush they had disarmed the English who were in charge and hoisted the Spanish flag once more. The *Santa Ana* was free, but she had to fight for life, a more desperate struggle perhaps than the first had been.

This bold attempt — one of the most honorable episodes of the battle of Trafalgar — was made on board a dismasted ship, that had lost her rudder, with half her complement of men killed or wounded, and the other half in a wretched condition both moral and physical. However, the deed once done we had to face the consequences; two Englishmen, considerably battered no doubt, fired on the *Santa Ana;* but the *Asís*, the *Montañes*, and the *Rayo* — three ships that had got off with

Gravina on the 21st — opportunely came to the
rescue, having come out with a view to recapturing the prizes. The brave cripples rushed into
the desperate action, with even more courage perhaps than into the former battle, for their un-
healed wounds spurred them to fury and they
seemed to fight with greater ardor in proportion
as they had less life to lose.

All the incidents of the dreadful 21st were repeated before my eyes; the enthusiasm was tremendous, but the hands were so few that twice
the will and energy were needed. This heroic
action fills indeed but a brief page in history, for,
by the side of the great event which is now known
as the Battle of Trafalgar, such details are dwarfed
or disappear altogether like a transcient spark in
a night of gloom and horror.

The next thing that happened to me person-
ally cost me some bitter tears. Not finding my
master at once I felt sure he was in some danger,
so I went down to the upper gun-deck and there
I found him, training a cannon. His trembling
hand had snatched the linstock from that of a
wounded sailor and he was trying, with the feeble
sight of his right eye, to discover to what point in
the foe he had better send the missile. When
the piece went off he turned to me trembling

with satisfaction, and said in a scarcely audible voice:

"Ah ha! Paca need not laugh at me now. We shall return to Cadiz in triumph."

Finally we won the fight. The English perceived the impossibility of recapturing the *Santa Ana* when, besides the three ships already mentioned, two other Frenchmen and a frigate came up to her assistance in the very thick of the fray.

We were free, and by a glorious effort; but at the very moment of victory we saw most clearly the peril we were in, for the *Santa Ana* was now so completely disabled that we could only be towed into Cadiz. The French frigate *Themis* sent a cable on board and put her head to the North, but what could she do with such a deadweight in tow as the *Santa Ana*, which could do little enough to help herself with the ragged sails that still clung to her one remaining mast? The other ships that had supported her — the *Rayo*, the *Montañés*, and the *San Francisco de Asís*, were forced to proceed at full sail to the assistance of the *San Juan* and the *Bahama*, which were also in the hands of the English. There we were, alone, with no help but the frigate that was doing her best for us — a child leading a giant. What would become of us if the enemy — as was very probable — recovering from their repulse, were to fall upon us with renewed energy and re-inforcements? However, Providence thought good to protect us; the wind favored us, and our frigate gently leading the way, we found ourselves nearing Cadiz.

Only five leagues from port! What an un-speakable comfort! Our miseries seemed ended; ere long we should set foot on *terra firma*, and though we brought news no doubt of a terrible disaster, we were bringing relief and joy to many faithful souls who were suffering mortal anguish in the belief that those who were returning alive and well had all perished.

The valor of the Spaniards did not avail to rescue any ships but ours, for they were too late and had to return without being able to give chase to the English ships that kept guard over the *San Juan*, the *Bahama*, and the *San Ildefonso*. We were still four leagues from land when we saw them making towards us. A southerly gale was blowing up and it was clear to all on board the *Santa Ana* that if we did not soon get into port we should have a bad time of it. Once more we were filled with anxiety; once more we lost hope almost in sight of safety, and when a few hours more on the cruel sea would have seen us safe and sound in harbor. Night was coming on black and angry; the sky was covered with dark clouds which seemed to lie on the face of the ocean, and the lurid flashes which lighted them up from time to time added terror to the gloom. The sea waxing in fury every instant, as if it were not yet satiated, raved and roared with hungry rage, demanding more and yet more victims. The remnant of the mighty fleet which a short time since had defied its fury combined with that of the foe was not to escape from the wrath of the angry element which, implacable as an ancient god and pitiless to the last, was as cruel to the victor as to the conquered.

I could read the signs of deep depression in the face not only of my master but of the Admiral, Alava, who, in spite of his wounds, still kept on his feet and signalled to the frigate to make all possible speed; but, instead of responding to his very natural haste, the *Themis* prepared to shorten sail so as to be able to keep before the gale. I shared the general dismay and could not help reflecting on the irony with which Fate mocks at our surest calculations and best founded hopes, on the swiftness with which she flings us from happy security to the depth of misery. Here we were, on the wide ocean, that majestic emblem of

OXFORD
WITHDRAWN

human life. A gust of wind and it is completely transformed, the light ripple which gently caressed the vessel's side swells into a mountain of water that lashes and beats it, the soft music of the wavelets in a calm turns to a loud, hoarse voice, threatening the frail bark which flings itself into the waters as though its keel were unable to balance it, to rise the next moment buffeted and tossed by the very wave that has lifted it from the abyss. A lovely day ends in a fearful night, or, on the other hand, a radiant moon that illumines an infinite sky and soothes the soul, pales before an angry sun at whose light all nature quakes with dismay.

We had experienced all these viscissitudes, and in addition, those which are the result of the will of man. We had suffered shipwreck in the midst of defeat; after escaping once we had been compelled to fight again, this time with success; and then, when we thought ourselves out of our troubles, when we hailed Cadiz with delight, we were once more at the mercy of the tempest which had treacherously deluded us only to destroy us outright. Such a succession of adverse fortune seemed monstrous — it was like the malignant aberrations of a divinity trying to do all the harm he could devise to us hapless mortals — but it was only the natural course of things at sea, combined with the fortune of war. Given a combination of these two fearful forces and none but an idiot can be astonished at the disasters that must ensue.

Another circumstance contributed to my master's distress of mind, and to mine too, that evening. Since the rescue of the *Santa Ana* Malespina had disappeared. At last, after seeking him everywhere, I discovered him lying in a heap on a sofa in the cabin. I went up to him and saw that he was very pale; I spoke to him but he could not answer. He tried to move but fell back gasping.

"Are you wounded?" I asked. "I will fetch some one to attend to you."

"It is nothing," he said. "Can you get me some water?"

I went at once for my master.

"What is the matter — this wound in your hand?" said he, examining the young officer.

"It is more than that," replied Don Rafael sadly, and he put his hand to his right side close by his sword-belt. And, then, as if the effort of pointing out his wound and speaking those few words had been too much for his weakened frame, he closed his eyes and neither spoke nor moved for some minutes.

"This is serious," said my master anxiously.

"It is more than serious," said a surgeon who

had come to examine him. Malespina, deeply depressed by finding himself in so evil a plight, and believing himself past all hope, had not even reported himself as wounded, but had crept away to this corner where he had given himself up to his reflections and memories. He believed that he was killed and he would not have the wound touched. The surgeon assured him that though it was dangerous it need not prove mortal, though he owned that if he did not get into port that night so that he might be properly treated on shore, his life, like that of the rest of the wounded, was in the greatest danger. The *Santa Ana* had lost ninety-seven men killed on the 21st, and a hundred and forty wounded ; all the resources of the surgery were exhausted and many indispensable articles were altogether wanting. Malespina's catastrophe was not the only one during the rescue, and it had been the will of Heaven that another man very near and dear to me should share his fate. Marcial had been wounded ; though at first his indomitable spirit had kept him up and he hardly felt the pain and depression, before long he submitted to be carried down into the cock-pit, confessing that he was very badly hit. My master sent a surgeon to attend to him, but all he would say was that the wound would have been trifling in a man of five-and-twenty — but Marcial was past sixty.

Meanwhile the *Rayo* passed to leeward and we hailed her. Alava begged her to enquire of the *Themis* whether the captain thought he could get us into Cadiz, and when he roundly said, No, the Admiral asked whether the *Rayo*, which was almost unharmed, expected to get in safely. Her captain thought she might and it was agreed that Gardoqui, who was severely wounded, and several others, should be sent on board her, among them Don Rafael Malespina. Don Alonso obtained that Marcial should also be transferred to her in consideration for his age which greatly aggravated his case, and he sent me, too, in charge of them as page or sick-nurse, desiring me never to lose sight of them for an instant till I saw them safe in the hands of their family, at Cadiz, or even at Vejer. I prepared to obey him, though I tried to persuade my master that he too ought to come on board the *Rayo* for greater safety, but he would not even listen to such a suggestion.

"Fate," he said, "has brought me on board this ship, and in it I will stay till it shall please God to save us or no. Alava is very bad, most of the officers are more or less hurt, and I may be able to be of some service here. I am not one of

those who run away from danger; on the contrary, since the defeat of the 21st I have sought it;
I long for the moment when my presence may
prove to be of some use. If you reach home before me, as I hope you will, tell Paca that a good
sailor is the slave of his country, that I am very
glad that I came — that I do not regret it — on
the contrary. Tell her that she is to be glad, too,
when she sees me, and that my comrades would
certainly have thought badly of me if I had not
come. How could I have done otherwise? You
— do you not think that I did well to come?"

"Of course, certainly," I replied, anxious to
soothe his agitation, "who doubts it?" For his
excitement was so great that the absurdity of
asking the opinion of a page-boy had not even
occurred to him.

"I see you are a reasonable fellow," he went
on, much comforted by my admission. "I see
you have a noble and patriotic soul. But Paca
never sees anything excepting through her own
selfishness, as she has a very odd temper and has
taken it into her head that fleets and guns are
useless inventions, she cannot understand why I...
In short, I know that she will be furious when she
sees me and then — as we have not won the battle,
she will say one thing and another — oh! she

will drive me mad! However, I will not mind her. You — what do you say? Was I not right to come?"

"Yes, indeed, I think so," I said once more: "You were very right to come. It shows that you are a brave officer."

"Well then go — go to Paca, go and tell her so, and you will see what she will say," he went on more excited than ever. "And tell her that I am safe and sound, and my presence here is indispensable. In point of fact, I was the principal leader in the rescue of the *Santa Ana*. If I had not trained those guns — who knows, who knows? You — what do you think? We may do more yet; if the wind favors us to-morrow morning we may rescue some more ships. Yes sir, for I have a plan in my head . . . We shall see, we shall see. And so good bye, my boy. Be careful of what you say to Paca."

"I will not forget," said I. "She shall know that if it had not been for you we should not have recaptured the *Santa Ana*, and that if you are lucky you may still bring a couple of dozen ships into Cadiz."

"A couple of dozen! — no man; that is a large number. Two ships, I say — or perhaps three. In short, I am sure I was right to join the fleet. She will be furious and will drive me mad when I get home again; but I was right, I say — I am sure I was right." With these words he left me and I saw him last sitting in a corner of the cabin. He was praying, but he told his beads with as little display as possible, for he did not choose to be detected at his devotions. My master's last speech had convinced me that he had lost his wits and, seeing him pray, I understood how his enfeebled spirit had struggled in vain to triumph over the exhaustion of age, and now, beaten in strife, turned to God for support and consolation. Doña Francisca was right; for many years my master had been past all service but prayer.

We left the ship according to orders. Don Rafael and Marcial with the rest of the wounded officers were carefully let down into the boats by the strong-armed sailors. The violence of the sea made this a long and difficult business, but at last it was done and two boat loads were pulled off to the *Rayo*. The passage, though short was really frightful; but at last, though there were moments when it seemed to me that we must be swallowed up by the waves, we got alongside of the *Rayo* and with great difficulty clambered on board.

CHAPTER XV.

"Out of the frying-pan into the fire," said Marcial, when they laid him down on deck "However, when the captain commands the men must obey. *Rayo* is an unlucky name for this cursed ship. They say she will be in Cadiz by midnight, and I say she won't. We shall see what we shall see."

"What do you say, Marcial? we shall not get in?" I asked in much alarm.

"You, master Gabrielito, you know nothing about such matters," said he.

"But when Don Alonso and the officers of the *Santa Ana* say that the *Rayo* will get in to-night... She must get in when they say she will."

"Do not you know, you little landlubber, that the gentlemen of the quarter-deck are far more often mistaken than we are in the fo'castle? If not, what was the admiral of the fleet about? — *Mr. Corneta* — devil take him! You see he had not brains enough to work a fleet. Do you suppose that if *Mr. Corneta* had asked my advice we should have lost the battle?"

" And you think we shall not get into Cadiz ?"

" I say this old ship is as heavy as lead itself and not to be trusted either. She rides the sea badly and will not answer her helm. Why, she is as lop-sided and crippled as I am! If you try to put her to port off she goes to starboard."

In point of fact the *Rayo* was considered by all as bad a ship as ever sailed. But in spite of that, in spite of her advanced age — for she had been afloat nearly fifty-six years — as she was still sound she did not seem to be in any danger though the gale increased in fury every minute, for we were almost close to port. At any rate, did it not stand to reason that the *Santa Ana* was in greater jeopardy, dismasted and ruddeless, in tow of a frigate ?

Marcial was carried to the cock-pit and Malespina to the captain's cabin. When we had settled him there, with the rest of the wounded officers, I suddenly heard a voice that was familiar to me though for the moment I could not identify it with any one I knew. However, on going up to the group whence the stentorian accents proceeded, drowning every other voice, what was my surprise at recognizing Don José Maria Malespina! I ran to tell him that his son was on board, and the worthy parent at once broke off the string of rodo-

montade that he was pouring forth and flew to the
wounded man. His delight was great at finding
him alive; he had come out of Cadiz because he
could no longer endure the suspense and he must
know what had become of his boy at any cost.

"Why your wound is a mere trifle," he said,
embracing his son. "A mere scratch! But you
are not used to wounds; you are quite a molly-
coddle, Rafael. Oh, if only you had been old
enough to go with me to fight in Rousillon! You
would have learnt there what wounds are — something like wounds! Do you know a ball hit me in
the fleshy part of the arm, ran up to my shoulder
and then right round the shoulder blade and out
by the belt. A most extraordinary case, that was.
But in three days I was all right again and commanding the artillery at Bellegarde." He went on
to give the following account of his presence on
board the *Rayo*.

"We knew the issue of the battle at Cadiz, by
the evening of the 21st. I tell you, gentlemen —
no one would listen to me when I talked of reforming our artillery and you see the consequences.
Well, as soon as I knew the worst and had learnt
that Gravina had come in with a few ships I went
to see if the *San Juan Nepomuceno*, on board
which you were, was one of them; but they told

me she had been captured. You cannot imagine
my anxiety; I could hardly doubt that you were
dead, particularly when I heard how many had been
killed on board your ship. However, I am one of
those men who must follow a matter up to the
end, and knowing that some of the ships in port
were preparing to put out to sea in hope of pick-
ing up derelicts and rescuing captured vessels, I
determined to set out without a moment's delay
and sail in one of them. I explained my wishes
to Solano and then to the Admiral in command,
my old friend Escaño, and after some hesitation
they allowed me on board. I embarked this morning, and enquired of every one in the *Rayo* for
some news of you and of the *San Juan*, but I
could get no comfort; nay, quite the contrary, for
I heard that Churruca was killed and that his ship,
after a glorious defence, had struck to the enemy.
You may fancy my anxiety. How far was I from
supposing this morning, when we rescued the
Santa Ana, that you were on board! If I had
but known it for certain I would have redoubled
my efforts in the orders I issued — by the kind
permission of these gentlemen; Alava's ship
should have been free in two minutes."

The officers who were standing round us looked
at each other with a shrug as they heard Don

José's last audacious falsehood. I could gather from their smiles and winks that he had afforded them much diversion all day with his vainglorious fictions, for the worthy gentleman could put no bridle on his indefatigable tongue, even under the most critical and painful circumstances.

The surgeon now said that his patients ought to be left to rest and that there must be no conversation in their presence, particularly no reference to the recent disaster. Don José Maria, however, contradicted him flatly, saying that it was good to keep their spirits up by talking to them.

"In the war in Rousillon," he added, "those who were badly wounded — and I was several times—sent for the soldiers to dance and play the guitar in the infirmary; and I am very certain that this treatment did more to cure us than all your plasters and dosing."

"Yes, and in the wars with the French Republic," said an Andalusian officer who wanted to trump Don José's trick, "it was a regular thing that a *corps de ballet* should be attached to the ambulance corps, and an opera company as well. It left the surgeons and apothecaries nothing to do, for a few songs, and a short course of pirouettes and capers set them to rights again, as good as new."

"Come, come !" cried Malespina, "this is too

much.   You do not mean to say that music and
dancing can heal a wound ?"

"You said so."

"Yes, but that was only once and it is not
likely to occur again.   Perhaps you think it not
unlikely that we may have such another war as
that in Rousillon ? The most bloody, the best conducted, the most splendidly planned war since
the days of Epaminondas! Certainly not. Every
thing about it was exceptional; and you may believe me when I say it, for I was in the thick of it,
from the Introit to the last blessing.   It is to my
experience there that I owe my knowledge of artillery — did you never hear me spoken of? I am
sure you must recognize my name.   Well, you
must know that I have in my head a magnificent
scheme, and if one of these days it is only realized
we shall hear of no more disasters like that of the
21st.   Yes, gentlemen," he said, looking round at
the three or four officers who were listening, with
consummate gravity and conceit: "Something
must be done for the country.   Something must
be devised — something stupendous, to recoup us
at once for our losses and secure victory to our
fleets for ever and ever, Amen."

"Let us hear, Don José," said one of the
audience.   "Explain your scheme to us."

"Well, I am devoting my mind to the construction of 300-pounders."

"Three-hundred-pounders!" cried the officers with shouts of laughter and derision. "Why, the largest we carry is a 36-pounder."

"Mere toys! Just imagine the ruin that would be dealt by a 300-pound gun fired into the enemy's fleet," said Malespina. "But what the devil is that?" he added putting out his hand to keep himself from falling, for the *Rayo* rolled so heavily that it was very difficult for any one to keep his feet.

"The gale is stiffening and I doubt our getting into Cadiz to-night," said one of the officers moving away. The worthy man had now but two listeners, but he proceeded with his mendacious harangue all the same.

"The first thing must be to build a ship from 95 to 100 yards in length."

"The Devil you will! That would be a snug little craft with a vengeance!" said one of the officers. "A hundred yards! Why the *Trinidad*— God rest her — was but seventy and everybody thought her too long. She did not sail well you know and was very difficult to handle."

"It does not take much to astonish you I see," Malespina went on. "What is a hundred yards? Why, much larger ships than that might be built.

And you must know that I would build her of iron."

" Of iron !" and his listeners went into fits of laughter.

"Yes sir, of iron. Perhaps you are not familiar with the science of hydrostatics ? There can be no difficulty in building an iron ship of 7000 tons."

" And the *Trinidad* was of 4000! and that was too big. But do you not see that in order to move such a monster you would want such gigantic tackle that no human power could work it ?"

" Not a bit of it! — Besides, my good sir, who told you that I was so stupid as to think that I could trust to the wind alone to propel my ship ? If you knew — I have an idea. — But I do not care to explain my scheme to you for you would not understand me."

At this point of his discourse Don José was so severely shaken that he fell on all fours. But not even this could stop his tongue. Another of his audience walked away, leaving only one who had to listen and to keep up the conversation.

" What a pitching and tossing," said the old man. " I should not wonder if we were driven on shore. — Well, as I was saying — I should move my monster by an invention of my own — can you guess what?—By steam. To this end I should construct a peculiar kind of machine in which the steam, expanding and contracting alternately inside two cylinders, would put certain wheels in motion; then . . . ."

The officer would listen no longer, and though he had no commission on board the ship nor any fixed duty, being one of the rescued, he went off to assist in working the ship, which was hard enough to do as the tempest increased. Malespina was left alone with me for an audience, and at first I thought he would certainly cease talking, not thinking me capable of sustaining the conversation. But, for my sins, it would seem that he credited me with more merit than I could lay claim to, for he turned to me and went on:

"You understand what I mean? Seven thousand tons, and steam working two wheels, and then . . . ."

"Yes señor, I understand you perfectly," I replied, to see if he would be silent, for I did not care to hear him, nor did the violent motion of the ship which threatened us with immediate peril at all incline my mind to dissertations on the aggrandizement of the Spanish navy.

"I see," he continued, "that you know how to appreciate me and value my inventions. You see at once that such a ship as I describe would be invincible, and as available for attack as for defence. With four or five discharges it could rout thirty of the enemy's ships."

"Would not their cannon do it some damage?" I asked timidly, and speaking out of civility rather than from any interest I felt in the matter.

"Your observation is a very shrewd one my little gentleman, and proves that you really appreciate my great invention. But to avoid injury from the enemy's guns I should cover my ship with thick plates of steel. I should put on it a breastplate, in fact, such as warriors wore of old. With this protection it could attack the foe, while their projectiles would have no more effect on its sides than a broadside of bread-pills flung by a child. It is a wonderful idea I can tell you, this notion of mine. Just fancy our navy with two or three ships of this kind! What would become of the English fleet then, in spite of its Nelsons and Collingwoods?"

"But they might make such ships themselves," I returned eagerly and feeling the force of this argument. "The English would do the same, and then the conditions of the battle would be equal again."

Don José was quite dumbfounded by this sug-

gestion and for a minute did not know what to
say, but his inexhaustible imagination did not de-
sert him for long and he answered, but somewhat
crossly :

"And who said, impertinent boy, that I
should be such a fool as to divulge the secret so
that the English might learn it ? These ships
would be constructed in perfect secrecy without
a word being whispered even to any one. Suppose a fresh war were to break out. We should
defy the English : 'Come on, gentlemen,' we
should say, 'we are ready, quite ready.' The
common ships would put out to sea and begin
the action when lo and behold ! out come two or
three of these iron monsters into the thick of the
fight, vomiting steam and smoke and turning here
and there without troubling themselves about the
wind ; they go wherever they are wanted, splin-
tering the wooden sides of the enemy's ships by
the blows of their sharp bows, and then with a
broadside or two... It would all be over in a
quarter of an hour."

I did not care to raise any further difficulties
for the conviction that our vessel was in the
greatest danger quite kept my mind from dwell-
ing on ideas so inappropriate to our critical situation. In fact, I never thought again of the mon-

ster ship of the old man's fancy till thirty years
after when we first heard of the application of
steam to purposes of navigation; and again when,
half-way through the century, our fine frigate the
Numancia actually realized the extravagant
dreams of the braggart of Trafalgar.

Half a century later I remembered Don José
Maria Malespina and I said: "He seemed to us a
bombastic liar; but conceptions which are extravagant in one place and time, when born in due
season become marvellous realities! And since
living to see this particular instance of the fact, I
have ceased to think any Utopia impossible, and
the greatest visionaries seem to me possible men
of genius."

I left Don José in the cabin and ascended the
companion-way, to see what was going forward,
and as soon as I was on deck I understood the
dangerous situation of the *Rayo*. The gale not
only prevented her getting into Cadiz, but was
driving her towards the coast where she must
inevitably be wrecked on the rocky shore. Melancholy as was the fate of the abandoned *Santa
Ana* it could not be more desperate than ours.
I looked with dismay into the faces of the officers
and crew to see if I could read hope in any one
of them, but despair was written in all. I glanced

at the sky—it was black and awful; I gazed at the sea—it was raging with fury. God was our only hope — and He had shown us no mercy since the fatal 21st!

The *Rayo* was running northwards. I could understand, from what I heard the men about me saying, that we were driving past the reef of Marajotes — past Hazte Afuera — Juan Bola — Torregorda, and at last past the entrance to Cadiz. In vain was every effort made to put her head round to enter the bay. The old ship, like a frightened horse, refused to obey; the wind and waves carried her on, due north, with irresistible fury and science could do nothing to prevent it.

We flew past the bay, and could make out to our right, Rota, Punta Candor, Punta de Meca, Regla and Chipiona. There was not a doubt that the *Rayo* must be driven on shore, close to the mouth of the Guadalquivir. I need hardly say that the sails were close reefed and that as this proved insufficient in such a furious tempest the topmasts were lowered; at last it was even thought necessary to cut away the masts to prevent her from foundering. In great storms a ship has to humble herself, to shrink from a stately tree to a lowly plant; and as her masts will no more yield than the branches of an oak, she is under the sad necessity of seeing them amputated and losing her limbs to save her life.

The loss of the ship was now inevitable. The main and mizzen-masts were cut through and sent overboard, and our only hope was that we might be able to cast anchor near the coast. The anchors were got ready and the chains and cables strengthened. We were now running right on shore, and two cannon were fired as a signal that we wanted help; for as we could clearly distinguish fires we kept up our hope that there must be some one to come to our rescue. Some were of opinion that a Spanish or English ship had already been wrecked here and that the fires we saw had been lighted by the destitute crew. Our anxiety increased every instant, and as for myself I firmly believed that I was face to face with a cruel death. I paid no attention to what was doing on board, being much too agitated to think of anything but my end, which seemed inevitable. If the vessel ran on a rock, what man could swim through the breakers that still divided us from the coast? The most dangerous spot in a storm is just where the waves are hurled revolving against the shore, as if they were trying to scoop it out and drag away whole tracts of earth into the gulfs below. The blow of a wave as it dashes forward and its gluttonous fury as it rushes back again, is such as no human strength can stand against.

At last, after some hours of mortal anguish, the keel of the *Rayo* came upon a sand bank and there she stuck. The hull and the remaining masts shivered as she struck; she seemed to be trying to cut her way through the obstacle ; but it was too much for her; after heaving violently for a few moments, her stern went slowly down with fearful creaks and groans, and she remained steady. All was over now, nothing remained to be done but to save ourselves by getting across the tract of sea which separated us from the land. This seemed almost impossible in the boats we had on board ; our best hope was that they might send us help from the shore, for it was evident that the crew of a lately wrecked vessel was encamped there, and one of the government cutters, which had been placed on the coast by the naval authorities for service in such cases, must surely be in the neighborhood. The *Rayo* fired again and again, and we watched with desperate impatience, for if some succour did not reach us soon we must all go down in the ship. The hapless crippled mass whose timbers had parted as she struck seemed likely to hasten her end by the violence of her

throes, and the moment could not be far off when
her ribs must fall asunder and we should be left
at the mercy of the waves with nothing to cling
to but the floating wreck.

Those on shore could do nothing for us, but by
God's mercy our signal guns were heard by a
sloop which had put to sea at Chipiona and which
now approached us, keeping, however, at a re-
spectful distance. As soon as her broad mainsail
came in view we knew that we were saved, and
the captain of the *Rayo* gave orders to insure our
all getting on board without confusion in. such
imminent peril. My first idea, when I saw the
boats being got out, was to run to the two men
who most interested me on board: Marcial and
young Malespina, both wounded, though Marcial's
was not a serious case. I found the young officer
in a very bad way and saying to the men around
him: "I will not be moved — leave me to die
here."

Marcial had crawled up on deck and was lying
on the planks so utterly prostrate and indifferent
that I was really terrified at his appearance. He
looked up as I went near him and taking my hand
said in piteous tones: "Gabrielillo, do not forsake
me !" .

"To land !" I cried trying to encourage him,

" we are all going on shore." But he only shook his head sadly as if he foresaw some immediate disaster.

I tried to help him up, but after the first effort he let himself drop as if he were dead. " I cannot," he said at length. The bandages had come off his wound and in the confusion of our desperate situation no one had thought of applying fresh ones. I dressed it as well as I could, comforting him all the time with hopeful words; I even went so far as to laugh at his appearance to see if that would rouse him. But the poor old man could not smile; he let his head droop gloomily on his breast, as insensible to a jest as he was to consolation. Thinking only of him, I did not observe that the boats were putting off. Among the first to be put on board were Don José Malespina and his son; my first impulse had been to follow them in obedience to my master's orders, but the sight of the wounded sailor was too much for me. Malespina could not need me, while Marcial was almost a dead man and still clung to my hand with his cold fingers, saying again and again : " Gabrielillo, do not leave me."

The boats labored hard through the breakers, but notwithstanding, when once the wounded had been moved the embarkation went forward rapidly, the sailors flinging themselves in by a rope or taking a flying leap. Several jumped into the water and saved themselves by swimming. It flashed through my mind as a terrible problem, by which of these means I could escape with my life, and there was no time tô lose for the *Rayo* was breaking up; the after-part was all under water and the cracking of the beams and timbers, which were in many places half rotten, warned me that the huge hulk would soon cease to exist. Every one was rushing to the boats, and the sloop, which kept at a safe distance, very skilfully handled so as to avoid shipping water, took them all on board. The empty boats came back at once and were filled again in no time.

Seeing the helpless state in which Marcial was lying I turned, half-choked with tears, to some sailors and implored them to pick him up and carry him to a boat; but it was as much as they could do to save themselves. In my desperation I tried to lift him and drag him to the ship's side, but my small strength was hardly enough to raise his helpless arms. I ran about the deck, seeking some charitable soul; and some seemed on the point of yielding to my entreaties, but their own pressing danger choked their kind impulses. To understand such cold-blooded cruelty you must have gone through such a scene of horror; every

feeling of humanity vanishes before the stronger
instinct of self-preservation which becomes a perfect possession, and sometimes reduces man to the
level of a wild beast.

"Oh the wretches! they will do nothing to
save you, Marcial," I cried in bitter anguish.

"Let them be," he said. "They are the same
at sea as on shore. But you child, be off, run, or
they will leave you behind." I do not know
which seemed to me the most horrible alternative
— to remain on board with the certainty of death,
or to go and leave the miserable man alone. At
length, however, natural instinct proved the
stronger and I took a few steps towards the ship's
side; but I turned back to embrace the poor old
man once more and then I ran as fast as I could
to the spot where the last men were getting into
the boat. There were but four, and when I
reached the spot I saw that all four had jumped
into the sea and were swimming to meet the boat
which was still a few yards distant.

"Take me!" I shrieked, seeing that they were
leaving me behind. "I am coming too!— Take
me too!"

I shouted with all my strength but they either
did not hear or did not heed me. Dark as it was,
I could make out the boat and even knew when

they were getting into it, though I could hardly say that I saw them. I was on the point of flinging myself overboard to take my chance of reaching the boat when, at that very moment, it had vanished — there was nothing to be seen but the black waste of waters. Every hope of escape had vanished with it. I looked round in despair — nothing was visible but the waves preying on what was left of the ship; not a star in the sky, not a spark on shore — the sloop had sailed away.

Beneath my feet, which I stamped with rage and anguish, the hull of the *Rayo* was going to pieces, nothing remained indeed but the bows, and the deck was covered with wreck; I was actually standing on a sort of raft which threatened every moment to float away at the mercy of the waves.

I flew back to Marcial. "They have left me, they have left us!" I cried. The old man sat up with great difficulty, leaning on one hand and his dim eyes scanned the scene and the darkness around us.

"Nothing . . ." he said. "Nothing to be seen; no boats, no land, no lights, no beach.— They are not coming back!"

As he spoke a tremendous crash was heard beneath our feet in the depths of the hold under the bows, long since full of water; the deck gave a great lurch and we were obliged to clutch at a capstan to save ourselves from falling into the sea. We could not stand up; the last remains of the *Rayo* were on the point of being engulfed. Still, hope never forsakes us; and I, at any rate, consoled myself with the belief that things might remain as they were now till day-break and with observing that the fore-mast had not yet gone overboard. I looked up at the tall mast, round which some tatters of sails and ends of ropes still flapped in the wind, and which stood like a dishevelled giant pointing heavenward and imploring mercy with the persistency of despair; and I fully determined that if the rest of the hull sank under water I would climb it for a chance of life.

Marcial laid himself down on the deck.

"There is no hope, Gabrielillo," he said. "They have no idea of coming back, nor could they if they tried in such a sea. Well, since it is God's will, we must both die where we are. For me, it matters not; I am an old man, and of no use for any earthly thing. — But you, you are a mere child and you ..." But here his voice broke with emotion. "You," he went on, "have no sins to answer for, you are but a child. But I ... Still, when a man dies like this — what shall I say — like a dog or a cat — there is no need, I have heard, for the priest to give him absolution — all that is needed is that he should make his peace himself with God. Have you not heard that said ?"

I do not know what answer I made ; I believe I said nothing, but only cried miserably.

"Keep your heart up, Gabrielillo," he went on. "A man must be a man, and it is at a time like this that you get to know the stuff you are made of. You have no sins to answer for, but I have. They say that when a man is dying and there is no priest for him to confess to, he ought to tell whatever he has on his conscience to any one who will listen to him. Well, I will confess to you Gabrielillo; I will tell you all my sins, and I expect God will hear me through you and then he will forgive me."

Dumb with terror and awe at the solemnity of his address, I threw my arms round the old man who went on speaking.

"Well, I say, I have always been a Christian, a Catholic, Apostolic Roman; and that I always was and still am devoted to the Holy Virgin del Cármen, to whom I pray for help at this very minute; and I say too that though for twenty years I have never been to confession nor received the sacrament, it has not been my fault, but that

of this cursed service, and because one always puts
it off from one Sunday to the next. But it is a
trouble to me now that I failed to do it, and I
declare and swear that I pray God and the Virgin
and all the Saints to punish me if it was my fault;
for this year, if I have never been to confession or
communion, it was all because of those cursed
English that forced me to go to sea again just
when I really meant to make it up with the
Church. I never stole so much as a pin's head,
and I never told a lie, except for the fun of it now
and then. I repent of the thrashings I gave my
wife thirty years ago — though I think she rightly
deserved them, for her temper was more venom-
ous than a scorpion's sting. I never failed to
obey the captain's order in the least thing; I hate
no one on earth but the 'great-coats,' and I should
have liked to see them made mince-meat of.
However, they say we are all the children of the
same God, so I forgive them, and I forgive the
French who brought us into this war. I will say
no more, for I believe I am going — full sail. I
love God and my mind is easy. Gabriel hold me
tight and stick close to me; you have no sins to
answer for, you will go straight away to Heaven
to pipe tunes with the angels. Ah well, it is
better to die so, at your age, than to stay below in

this wicked world.   Keep up your courage, boy,
till the end.   The sea is rising and the *Rayo* will
soon be gone.   Death by drowning is an easy
one ; do not be frightened — stick close to me.
In less than no time we shall be out of it all ; I
answering to God for all my shortcomings, and
you as happy as a fairy, dancing through the
star-paved heavens—and they tell us happiness
never comes to an end up there because it is
eternal, or, as they say, to-morrow and to-morrow
and to-morrow, world without end ...."

He could say no more.   I clung passionately
to the poor mutilated body.   A tremendous sea
swept over the bows and I felt the water dash
against my shoulder.   I shut my eyes and fixed
my thoughts on God.   Then I lost consciousness
and knew no more.

CHAPTER XVI.

WHEN, I know not how long after, the idea of life dawned once more on my darkened spirit, I was conscious only of being miserably cold; indeed, this was the only fact that made me aware of my own existence, for I remembered nothing whatever of all that had happened and had not the slightest idea of where I was. When my mind began to get clearer and my senses recovered their functions I found that I was lying on the beach; some men were standing round me and watching me with interest. The first thing I heard was: ".Poor little fellow ! — he is coming round."

By degrees I recovered my wits and, with them, my recollection of past events. My first· thought was for Marcial, and I believe that the first words I spoke were an enquiry for him. But no one could tell me anything about him; I recognized some of the crew of the *Rayo* among the men on the beach and asked them where he was; they were all agreed that he must have perished. Then I wanted to know how I had been saved, but they would tell me nothing about that either. They gave me some liquor to drink, I know not what, and carried me to a neighboring hut, where, warmed by a good fire and cared for by an old woman, I soon felt quite well, though still rather weak. Meanwhile I learnt that another cutter had put out to reconnoitre the wreck of the *Rayo* and that of a French ship which had met with the same fate, and that they had picked me up still clinging to Marcial; they found that I could be saved but my companion was dead. I learnt too that a number of poor wretches had been drowned in trying to reach the coast. Then I wanted to know what had become of Malespina, but no one knew anything either of him or of his father. I enquired about the *Santa Ana* which, it appeared, had reached Cadiz in safety, so I determined to set out forthwith to join my master. We were at some distance from Cadiz, on the coast to the north of the Guadalquivir, I wanted therefore to start at once to make so long a journey. I took two days' rest to recover my strength, and then set out for Sanlúcar, in the company of a sailor who was going the same way. We crossed the river on the morning of the 27th and then continued our walk, keeping along the coast. As my companion was a jolly, friendly fellow the journey was as pleasant as I could expect in the frame of mind I was in, grieved at Marcial's death and depressed by the scenes I had so lately witnessed. As we walked on we discussed the battle and the shipwrecks that had ensued.

"A very good sailor was that old cripple," said my companion. "But what possessed him to go to sea again with more than sixty years on his shoulders? It served him right to come to a bad end."

"He was a brave seaman," said I, "and had such a passion for fighting that even his infirmities could not keep him quiet when he had made up his mind to join the fleet."

"Well, I have had enough of it for my part," said the sailor. "I do not want to see any more fighting at sea. The King pays us badly, and then, if you are maimed or crippled — good-bye to you — I know nothing about you — I never set eyes on you in my life.— Perhaps you don't believe me when I tell you the King pays his men so badly? But I can tell you this: most of the officers in command of the ships that went into action on the 21st had seen no pay for months. Only last year there was a navy captain at Cadiz who went as waiter in an inn because he had no other way of keeping himself or his children. His friends found him out though he tried to conceal his misery, and they succeeded at last in getting him out of his degrading position. Such things do not happen in any other country in the world; and then we are horrified at finding ourselves beaten by the English! As to the arsenals, I will say nothing about them; they are empty and it is of no use to hope for money from Madrid — not a *cuarto* comes this way. All the King's revenues are spent in paying the court officials, and chief among them the Prince of Peace, who gets 40,000 dollars as Counsellor of the Realm, Secretary of State, Captain-General, and Sergeant-Major of the Guards.— No, say I, I have had enough of serving the King. I am going home to my wife and children, for I have served my time and in a few days they must give me my papers."

"But you have nothing to complain of friend," said I, "since you were on board the *Rayo* which hardly did any fighting."

"I was not in the *Rayo* but in the *Bahama*, one of the ships that fought hardest and longest."

"She was taken and her captain killed, if I remember rightly."

"Aye, so it was," he said. "I could cry over it when I think of him — Don Dionisio Alcalá Galiano, the bravest seaman in the fleet. Well, he was a stern commander; he never overlooked the smallest fault, and yet his very severity made us love him all the more, for a captain who is feared for his severity — if his severity is unfailingly just—inspires respect and wins the affection of his men.   I can honestly say that a more noble and generous gentleman than Don Dionisio Alcalá Galiano was never born.   And when he wanted to do a civility to his friends he did not do it by halves; once, out in Havana he spent ten thousand dollars on a supper he gave on board ship."

"He was a first-rate seaman too, I have heard."

"Ah, that he was.   And he was more learned than Merlin and all the Fathers of the Church. He made no end of maps, and discovered Lord knows how many countries out there, where it is as hot as hell itself!   And then they send men like these out to fight and to be killed like a parcel of cabin-boys.   I will just tell you what happened on board the *Bahama*.   As soon as the fighting began Don Dionisio Alcalá Galiano knew we must be beaten on account of that infernal trick of turning the ships round — we were in the reserve and had been in the rear.   Nelson, who was certainly no fool, looked along our line, and he said : ' If we cut them through at two separate points, and keep them between two fires, hardly a ship will escape me.' And so he did, blast him; and as our line was so long the head could never help the tail. He fought us in detachments, attacking us in two wedge-shaped columns which, as I have heard say, were the tactics adopted by the great Moorish general, Alexander the Great, and now used by Napoleon. It is very certain, at any rate, that they got round us and cut us in three, and fought us ship to ship in such a manner that we could not support or help each other; every Spaniard had to deal with three or four Englishmen.

"Well, so you see the *Bahama* was one of the first to be under fire. Galiano reviewed the crew at noon, went round the gun-decks, and made us a speech in which he said: 'Gentlemen, you all know that our flag is nailed to the mast.' Yes, we all knew the sort of man our Captain was, and we were not at all surprised to hear it. Then he turned to the captain of the marines, Don Alonso Butron, 'I charge you to defend it,' he said. 'No Galiano ever surrenders and no Butron should either.'

"'What a pity it is,' said I, 'that such men should not have had a leader worthy of such courage, since they could not themselves conduct the fleet.'

"Aye, it is a pity, and you shall hear what happened. The battle began, and you know something of what it was like if you were on board the *Trinidad.* The ships riddled us with broadsides to port and starboard. The wounded fell like flies from the very first, and the captain first had a bad bruise on his foot and then a splinter struck his head and hurt him badly. But do you think he would give in, or submit to be plastered with ointment? Not a bit of it; he staid on the quarter-deck, just as if nothing had happened, though many a man he loved truly fell close to him never to stand up again. Alcalá Galiano gave his orders and directed his guns as if we had been firing a salute at a review. A spent ball knocked his telescope out of his hand and that made him laugh. I fancy I can see him now; the blood from his wound stained his uniform and his hands and he cared no more than if it had been drops of saltwater splashed up from the sea. He was a man of great spirit and a hasty temper; he shouted out his orders so positively that if we had not obeyed them because it was our duty, we should have done so out of sheer alarm. — But suddenly it was all over with him. — He was struck in the head by a shot and instantly killed.

"The fight was not at an end, but all our heart in it was gone. When our beloved captain fell the officers covered his body that we men might not see it, but we all knew at once what had happened, and after a short and desperate struggle for the honor of our flag, the *Bahama* surrendered to the English who carried her off to Gibraltar if she did not go to the bottom on the way, as I rather suspect she did."

After giving this history and telling me how he had been transferred from the *Bahama* to the *Santa Ana*, my companion sighed deeply and was silent for some time. However, as the way was long and dull I tried to reopen the conversation and I began telling him what I myself had seen, and how I had at last been put on board the *Rayo* with young Malespina.

"Ah!" said he. "Was he a young artillery officer who was transferred to the sloop to be taken to shore on the night of the 23d?"

"The very same," said I. "But no one has been able to tell me for certain what became of him."

"He was one of a party in the second boat which could not get to shore; some of those who were whole and strong contrived to escape, and among them that young officer's father; but all the wounded were drowned, as you may easily suppose, as the poor souls of course could not swim to land."

I was shocked to hear of Don Rafael's death,
and the thought of the grief it would be to my
hapless and adored little mistress quite overcame
me, choking every mean and jealous feeling.

"What a dreadful thing!" I exclaimed. "And
is it my misfortune to have to carry the news to
his sorrowing friends? But, tell me, are you certain of the facts?"

"I saw his father with my own eyes, lamenting
bitterly and telling all the details of the catastrophe with such distress it was enough to break
your heart. From what he said he seemed to
have saved everybody on board the boat, and he
declared that if he had saved his son it would have
been at the cost of the lives of all the others, so
he chose, on the whole, to preserve the lives of the
greatest number, even in sacrificing that of his son,
and he did so. He must be a singularly humane
man, and wonderfully brave and dexterous." But
I was so deeply distressed that I could not discuss
the subject. Marcial dead, Malespina dead! What
terrible news to take home to my master's house.
For a moment my mind was almost made up not
to return to Cadiz; I would leave it to chance or to
public rumor to carry the report to the sad hearts
that were waiting in such painful suspense. However, I was bound to present myself before Don

Alonso and give him some account of my proceedings.

At length we reached Rota and there embarked
for Cadiz. It is impossible to describe the commotion produced by the report of the disaster to
our fleet. News of the details had come in by degrees, and by this time the fate of most of our
ships was known, though what had become of
many men and even whole crews had not been as-
certained. The streets were full of distressing
scenes at every turn, where some one who had
come off scot-free stood telling off the deaths he
knew of, and the names of those who would be
seen no more. The populace crowded down to the
quays to see the wounded as they came on shore,
hoping to recognize a father, husband, son or
brother. There were episodes of frantic joy mingled with shrieks of dismay and bitter cries of dis-
appointment. Too often were hopes deceived and
fears confirmed, and the losers in this fearful lottery
were far more numerous than the winners. The
bodies thrown up on the shore put an end to the
suspense of many families, while others still hoped
to find those they had lost among the prisoners
taken to Gibraltar.

To the honor of Cadiz be it said never did a
community devote itself with greater willingness

to the care of the wounded, making no distinctions between friends and foes but hoisting the standard, as it were, of universal and comprehensive charity. Collingwood, in his narrative, does justice to this generosity on the part of my fellow-countrymen. The magnitude of the disaster had deadened all resentment, but is it not sad to reflect that it is only in misfortune that men are truly brothers?

In Cadiz I saw collected in the harbor the whole results of the conflict which previously, as an actor in it, I had only partially understood, since the length of the line and the manœuvring of the vessels would not allow me to see everything that happened. As I now learnt — besides the *Trinidad* — the *Argonauta*, 92 guns, Captain Don Antonio Pareja, and the *San Augustin*, 80 guns, Don Felipe Cagigal, had been sunk. Gravina had got back into Cadiz with the *Príncipe de Astúrias*, as well as the *Montañes*, 80 guns, commanded by Alcedo, who with his second officer Castaños, had been killed; the *San Justo*, 76 guns, Captain Don Miguel Gaston; the *San Leandro*, 74, Captain Don José Quevedo; the *San Francisco*, 74, Don Luis Flores; and the *Rayo*, 100, commanded by Macdonell. Four of these had gone out again on the 23d to recapture the vessels making for Gibraltar; and of these, two, the *San*

16

Francisco and the *Rayo* were wrecked on the coast. So, too, was the *Monarca*, 74 guns, under Argumosa, and the *Neptuno*, 80 guns; and her heroic commander, Don Cayetano Valdés, who had previously distinguished himself at Cape St. Vincent, narrowly escaped with his life. The *Bahama* had surrendered but went to pieces before she could be got into Gibraltar; the *San Ildefonso*, 74 guns, Captain Vargas, was taken to England, while the *San Juan Nepomuceno* was left for many years at Gibraltar, where she was regarded as an object of veneration and curiosity. The *Santa Ana* had come safely into Cadiz the very night we were taken off her.

The English too lost some fine ships, and not a few of their gallant officers shared Nelson's glorious fate.

With regard to the French it need not be said that they had suffered as severely as we had. With the exception of the four ships that withdrew under Dumanoir without showing fight — a stain which the Imperial navy could not for a long time wipe out — our allies behaved splendidly. Villeneuve, only caring to efface in one day the remembrance of all his mistakes, fought desperately to the last and was carried off a prisoner to Gibraltar. Many of their officers were taken with him, and very many were killed. Their vessels shared all our risks and dangers; some got off with Gravina, some were taken and several were wrecked on the coast. The *Achille* blew up, as I have said, in the midst of the action.

But in spite of all these disasters, Spain had paid dearer for the war than her haughty ally. France had lost the flower of her navy indeed, but at that very time Napoleon had won a glorious victory on land. His army had marched with wonderful rapidity from the shores of the English Channel across Europe, and was carrying out his colossal schemes in the campaign against Austria. It was on the 20th of October, the day before Trafalgar, that Napoleon, at the camp at Ulm, looked on as the Austrian troops marched past, while their officers delivered up their swords; only two months later, on the 2d of December, he won, on the field of Austerlitz, the greatest of his many victories.

These triumphs consoled France for the defeat of Trafalgar; Napoleon silenced the newspapers, forbidding them to discuss the matter; and when the victory of his implacable enemies, the English, was reported to him he simply shrugged his shoulders and said: "I cannot be everywhere at once."

CHAPTER XVII.

I POSTPONED the fatal hour when I must face my master as long as possible, but at last my destitute condition, without money and without a home, brought me to the point. As I went to the house of Doña Flora my heart beat so violently that I had to stop for breath at every step. The terrible shock I was about to give the family by announcing young Malespina's death weighed so terribly on my soul that I could not have felt more crushed and guilty if I had myself been the occasion of it. At last however, I went in. My presence in the court-yard caused an immense sensation. I heard heavy steps hurrying along the upper galleries and I had not been able to speak a word before I felt myself in a close embrace. I at once recognized Doña Flora, with more paint on her face than if it had been a picture, but seriously discomposed in effect by the good old soul's delight at seeing me once more. But all the fond names she lavished on me — her dear boy, her pet, her little angel — could not make me smile. I went up stairs, every one was in a bustle of excitement. I heard my master exclaim: "Oh! thank God! he is safe." I went into the drawing-room, and there it was Doña Francisca who came forward, asking with mortal anxiety — "And Don Rafael? — Where is Don Rafael?"

But for some minutes I could not speak; my voice failed me, I had not courage to tell the fatal news. They questioned me eagerly and I saw Doña Rosita come in from an adjoining room, pale, heavy-eyed, and altered by the anguish she had gone through. At the sight of my young mistress I burst into tears, and there was then no need for words. Rosita gave a terrible cry and fell senseless; her father and mother flew to her side, smothering their own grief, while Doña Flora melted into tears and took me aside to assure herself that I, at any rate, had returned whole in every part.

"Tell me," she said, "how did he come by his death? I felt sure of it — I told Paca so; but she would only say her prayers and believed that so she could save him. As if God could be troubled with such matters.— And you are safe and sound — what a comfort! No damage anywhere?"

It is impossible to describe the consternation

of the whole household. For a quarter of an hour nothing was to be heard but crying, lamentation, and sobbing; for Malespina's mother had come to Cadiz and was also in the house. But how mysterious are the ways of Providence in working out its ends! About a quarter of an hour, as I say, had elapsed since I had told them the news when a loud assertive voice fell on my ear. It was that of Don José Maria, shouting in the court-yard, calling his wife, Don Alonso, and Rosita. That which first struck me was that his tones seemed just as strident and cheerful as ever, which I thought very indecorous after the misfortune that had happened. We all ran to meet him, and I stared to see him radiant and smiling.

"But poor Don Rafael . . ." said my master.

"Safe and sound," replied Don José. "That is to say not exactly sound, but out of danger, for his wound is nothing to be anxious about. The fool of a surgeon said he would die, but I knew better. What do I care for surgeons! I cured him, gentlemen—I, I myself, by a new treatment which no one knows of but myself."

These words, which so suddenly and completely altered the aspect of affairs, astounded the audience. The greatest joy took the place of grief and dismay; and to wind up, as soon as their agitation allowed them to think of the delusion they had suffered under, they scolded me soundly for the fright I had given them. I excused myself by saying that I had only repeated the tale as it was told to me, and Don José flew into a great rage, calling me a rascal, an imposter, and a busybody.

It was happily true that Don Rafael was alive and out of danger; he had remained with some friends at Sanlúcar while his father had come to Cadiz to fetch his mother to see him. My readers will hardly believe in the origin of the mistake which had led me to announce the young man's death in such perfect good faith; though a few may have been led to suspect that some tremendous fib of the old man's must have given rise to the report that reached me. And so it was, neither more nor less. I heard all about it at Sanlúcar whither I went with the family. Don José Maria had invented a whole romance of devotion and skill on his own part, and had related more than once the history of his son's death, inventing so many dramatic details that for a few days he figured as a hero, and had been the object of universal admiration for his humanity and courage. His story was that the boat had upset, and that as the choice lay between rescuing his son and saving all the others he had chosen the latter alternative as the most magnanimous and philanthropical. This romance he dressed up in so many interesting, and at the same time probable circumstances that it could not fail to be believed. The falsehood was of course very soon found out, and his success was of brief duration, but not before the story had come to my ears and put me under the necessity of reporting it to the family. Though I knew very well how absolutely mendacious old Malespina could be, I had never dreamed of his lying about so serious a matter.

When all this excitement was over my master sank into deep melancholy; he would scarcely speak and seemed as though his soul, having no illusions left, had closed accounts with the world and was only waiting to take its departure. The absence of Marcial was to him the loss of the only companion of his childish old age; he had no one now to fight mimic battles with, and he gave himself up to dull sorrow. Nor did Doña Francisca spare him any drop of mortification, seeing him in this crest-fallen state. I heard her the same day saying spitefully:

"A pretty mess you have made of it! What do you think of yourself now? Now are you satisfied? Go, oh go by all means and join the fleet! Was I right or was I wrong? If you would only have listened to me. But you have had a lesson I hope; you see now how God has punished you."

"Woman, leave me in peace," said my master sadly.

"And now we are left without any fleet at all, and without sailors, and we shall soon find ourselves ruined out of hand if we keep up our alliance with the French. — Please God those gentry may not pay us out for their misfortunes. Señor Villeneuve! — he has covered himself with glory indeed! And Gravina again! If he had opposed the scheme of taking the fleet out, as Churruca and Alcalá Galiano did, he might have prevented this heartbreaking catastrophe."

"Woman, woman — what do you know about it? Do not annoy me," said Don Alonso quite vexed.

"What do I know about it? More than you do. Yes — I repeat it: Gravina may be a worthy gentleman and as brave as you please; but in this case, much good he has done!"

"He did his duty. You would have liked us all to be set down as cowards, I suppose?"

"Cowards, no — but prudent. It is as I say and repeat: the fleet ought never to have gone out of Cadiz just to humor the whims and conceit of Villeneuve.

"Every one here knew that Gravina, like the others, was of opinion that it ought to stop in the bay. But Villeneuve had made up his mind to it, intending to hit a blow that might restore him to his master's favor, and he worked on our Spanish pride. It seems that one of the reasons Gravina gave was the badness of the weather, and that he said, looking at the barometer in the cabin: 'Do you not see that the barometer foretells foul weather? Do you not see how it has gone down?' And then Villeneuve said drily: 'What is gone down here is courage!' At such an insult Gravina stood up, blind with rage, and threw the French Admiral's own conduct at Finisterre in his teeth. Some angry words were spoken on both sides and at last our Admiral exclaimed: 'To sea then to-morrow morning.'

"But I say that Gravina ought to have taken no notice of Villeneuve's insolence — none whatever; that prudence is an officer's first duty, and particularly when he knew — as we all knew —

that the fleet was not in a condition to fight the English.''

This view, which at the time seemed to me an insult to our national honor, I understood later was well-founded. Doña Francisca was right. Gravina ought not to have given way to Villeneuve's obstinacy, and I say it almost dims the halo of prestige with which the popular voice crowned the leader of the Spanish forces on that disastrous occasion. Without denying Gravina's many merits, in my opinion there was much exaggeration in the high-flown praises that were lavished upon him, both after the battle, and again when he died of his wounds a few months later.* Everything he did proved him to be an accomplished gentleman and a brave sailor, but he was perhaps too much of a courtier to show the determination which commonly comes of long experience in war; he was deficient too in that complete superiority which, in so learned a profession as the Navy, can only be acquired by assiduous study of the sciences on which it relies. Gravina was a good commander of a division under superior orders, but nothing more. The foresight, coolness, and immovable determination, which are indispensable elements in the man whose fortune it is to wield such

* March, 1806.

mighty forces, he had not; Don Cosme Damian
Churruca had—and Don Dionisio Alcalá Galiano.

My master made no reply to Doña Francisca's
last speech and when she left the room I observed
that he was praying as fervently as when I had
left him in the cabin of the *Santa Ana*. Indeed,
from that day Don Alonso did nothing else but
pray; he prayed incessantly till the day came
when he had to sail in the ship that never comes
home.

He did not die till some time after his daughter's marriage with Don Rafael Malespina, an
event which took place two months after the action which the Spanish know as "the 21st," and
the English as the battle of Trafalgar. My young
mistress was married one lovely morning, though
it was winter time, and set out at once for Medina-
Sidonia where a house was ready and waiting for
the young couple. I might look on at her happiness during the days preceding the wedding but
she did not observe the melancholy that I was suffering under; nor, if she had, would she have
guessed the cause. She thought more of herself
every day, as I could see, and I felt more and
more humiliated by her beauty and her superior
position in life. But I had taught myself to understand that such a sweet vision of all the graces

could never be mine, and this kept me calm; for
resignation — honest renunciation of all hope — is
a real consolation, though it is a consolation akin
to death.

Well, they were married, and the very day they
had left us for Medina-Sidonia Doña Francisca
told me that I was to follow them and enter their
service. I set out that night, and during my soli-
tary journey I tried to fight down my thoughts
and my feelings which wavered between accepting
a place in the house of the bridegroom or flying
from them forever. I arrived very early in the
morning and found out the house. I went into the
garden but on the bottom step I stopped, for my
reflections absorbed all my energies, and I had to
stand still to think more clearly; I must have stood
there for more than half an hour.

Perfect silence prevailed. . The young couple
were sleeping untroubled by a care or a sorrow. I
could not help recalling that far-off time when my
young mistress and I had played together. To me
she had then been my first and only thought. To
her, though I had not been the first in her affec-
tions, I had been something she loved and that she
missed if we were apart for an hour. In so short a
time how great a change!

I looked round me and all I saw seemed to

symbolize the happiness of the lovers and to mock my forlorn fate. Although it was winter time, I could picture the trees in full leaf, and the porch in front of the door seemed suddenly overgrown with creepers to shade them when they should come out. The sun was warmer, the air blew softer round this nest for which I myself had carried the first straws when I served as the messenger of their loves. I seemed to see the bare rosebushes covered with roses, the orange-trees with blossoms and fruit pecked by crowds of birds thus sharing in the wedding feast. My dreams and reflections were at last interrupted by a fresh young voice breaking the silence of the place and which made me tremble from head to foot as I heard it. It thrilled me with an indescribable sensation, that clear, happy, happy voice — whether of fear or shame I can hardly say; all I am sure of is that a sudden impulse made me turn from the door, and fly from the spot like a thief afraid of being caught.

My mind was made up. I quitted Medina-Sidonia forthwith, quite determined never to be a servant in that house, nor to return to Vejer. After a few minutes reflection I set out for Cadiz intending to get from thence to Madrid; and this was what I ultimately did, in spite of the persuasions of Doña Flora who tried to chain me to her side with a wreath of the faded flowers of her affection !

But since that day how much I have gone through ; how much I have seen, well worthy of record. My fate, which had taken me to Trafalgar, led me subsequently through many glorious and inglorious scenes, all in their way worth remembering. If the reader cares to hear the story of my life I will tell him more about it at a future opportunity.

END OF TRAFALGAR.

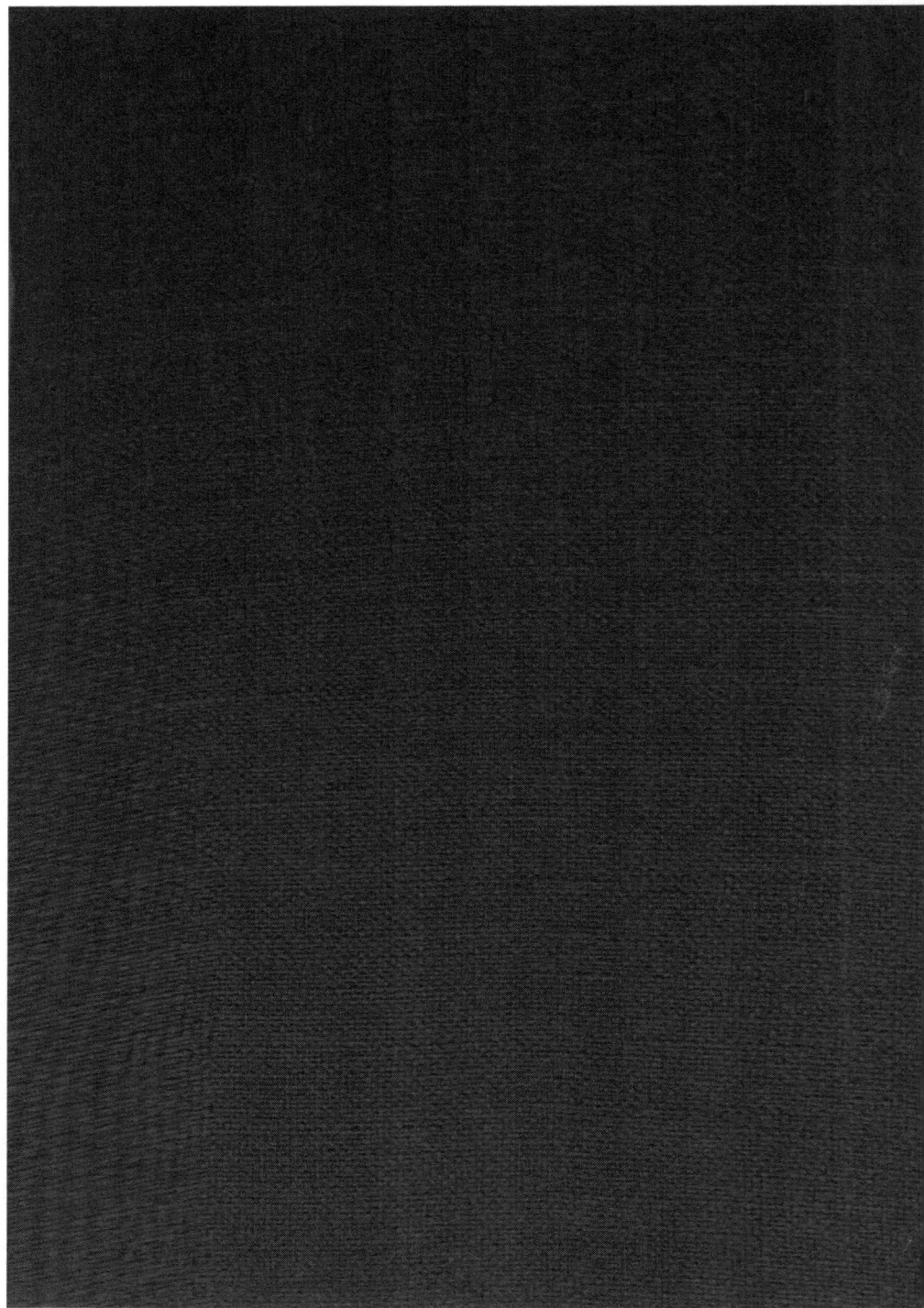

Ingram Content Group UK Ltd.
Milton Keynes UK
UKHW021959150623
423530UK00005B/117

9 781015 907928